THE I.T. LEADERS' HANDBOOK

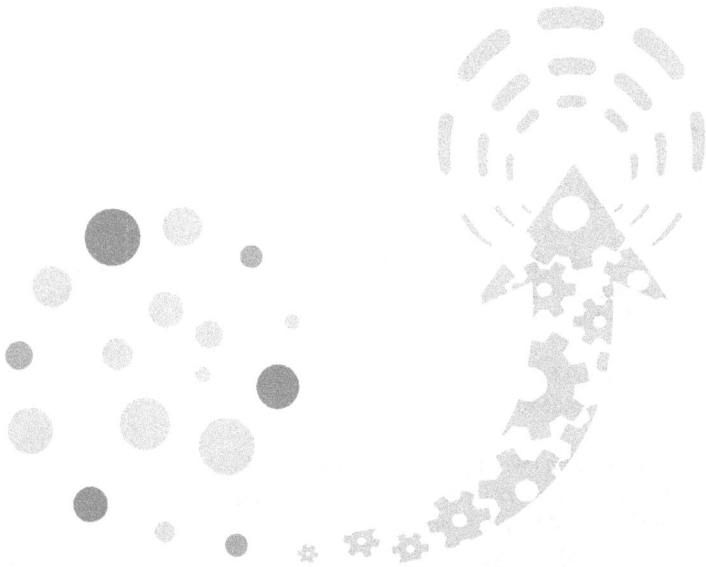

FOUNDATIONS FOR LEADING

THE INFORMATION TECHNOLOGY

DEPARTMENT

JOHN A. BREDESEN

Kennd

Kennd

Kennd Publishing
kennd-publishing.com

ISBN: 978-1-7366500-0-4
ISBN ebook: 978-1-7366500-1-1

Editor: Kristin Erlandsen (WritingwithKristin.com)
Cover Art & Illustrations: Dex Greenbright (DexGreenbright.com)
Fonts: Adobe Garamond Pro, Proxima Nova

Publisher's Notes:
- Web sites used as links or references may change after publication.
- Search terms will return results that change over time. The publisher and author expect the reader to use good judgment to choose appropriate results to learn the concepts.
- Advice provided in this book may not be appropriate in your situation. Good judgment is required when applying any advice received from a book.

Library of Congress Control Number: 2021903488

Printed in the United States
First Edition
10 9 8 7 6 5 4 3 2 1

Dedication

This book is dedicated to the hundreds of IT professionals I have worked with over the years. You have taught me so much as we worked to make our organizations successful.

CONTENTS

INTRODUCTION

Organizations structure themselves, in part, to manage people (HR), money (Finance), and technology (IT). These departments understand the details of their areas and how their work contributes to the success of the organization.

The Information Technology (IT) department lives at the intersection of the organization and the technological world.

It is often a thankless job.

The criticisms are many. IT is too slow to roll out changes. IT is too rigid with its rules and processes. IT is too expensive. IT has a huge backlog. IT is working on the wrong things.

Or so the organization believes.

As leaders of the IT department, it is our responsibility to run the department to meet the needs of the organization. Unfortunately, even with the best of efforts, the perception of the organization never matches our own. Even worse, sometimes the perception is correct.

There are a lot of books, magazines, websites, and individual postings aimed at the IT professional. But few of them address the larger problems organizations care about. There is significant information about specific technologies, but not much on how to lead an IT department.

Since I couldn't find such a book, I wrote it. This book is a collection of the scars and skills that I have earned over the years. If I had this book at the beginning of my IT career, I would have made far fewer mistakes.

I structure the book in four parts:

Part 1: Foundations

This part covers some basic concepts that apply throughout the rest of the book.

The *Square Root of Change* discusses important aspects of change management. Don't worry, there is no math.

> *If I had this book at the beginning of my IT career, I would have made far fewer mistakes.*

Focus & Finish is an approach that helps with the massive backlog all IT departments have. All that multi-tasking that you and your teams do to keep things moving? Well, stop it — it is hurting more than helping.

Risk Management is an under-appreciated skill for IT leaders. We are constantly evaluating risks. In fact, most of our decisions are about risk mitigation. The old adage about "no risk, no reward" is true, but it is better if we aren't stupid about it.

Next, we look at how *Proactivity Is Overrated*, and how our ability to react quickly and accurately needs more attention.

Finally, I look at the concept of *Technical Debt*. The concept has been around since at least the early 1990s, and I strongly encourage you to read the Wikipedia article (https://en.wikipedia.org/wiki/Technical_debt) if you aren't familiar with the concept. The "See Also" links on that page are pretty amusing. Fighting the good fight against Technical Debt is worth the effort.

Part 2: Business

If you read only one part of this book, read this one. Your most important job as an IT leader is to know the business. You can (and should!) have team members that know technology better than you. And, hopefully, you have some people skills to run a department. However, you must be the expert on the business in the IT department. Your team is busy doing other things; they need you to understand the bigger picture.

The bigger picture includes the entire organization and the environment that it operates in. Our job leading IT includes knowing and communicating how the organization should think about IT.

Also, no conversation about IT is complete without talking about Business Processes. This is the primary reason for IT to exist.

This part ends with two chapters about the work we do. Remember the backlog I mentioned above? Do you know for a fact that the IT department is working on the tasks that are most important to the organization? These chapters present some thoughts about prioritization and provide several methods for prioritizing the work.

Part 3: People
The IT department can't do anything without people. There are many books and resources that cover leadership. Find the ones that make sense for you and use them.

However, the pressures of the IT department and the servant mentality found in many IT staff create some unique challenges. This part of the book addresses those challenges.

I start with a chapter on *Managing Ourselves*. The airlines have it right when they advise us to "put on our own oxygen mask before helping others." If we don't do a good job of managing ourselves, how can we expect to do a good job of leading others?

Leading the IT team requires building on the strengths of the team. It requires that you trust your team. And it requires that you drive for continuous improvement.

Building the Right Team covers the attributes I have found helpful. There will always be good people that are exceptions to the list, so use it as a guide, not a rulebook.

Part 4: Technology

If you are looking to learn the latest technology, this is not the book you should be reading. This part goes over how to think about technology, but it doesn't cover the technology itself.

It kicks off with the question, *How Technical Do We Need To Be?* and then moves into managing our *Technology Portfolio*. Both are journeys and not just a static view.

Technology We Buy comes next. Spoiler: your selection process matters less than you think it does. And, of course, we need to think about *Technology We Build*, specifically custom applications. There is a time and a place for it, and this chapter covers how to do it right.

This part of the book wraps up with two fun chapters. The first is on *Shadow IT*. Some view it as a problem, others view it as an annoyance. I view it as an opportunity. The second covers *When We Don't Need Technology*. Yes, there are places in our organizations where technology is not the answer.

I have loved my twenty-five years of IT experience. The challenges of both technology and business have never been boring. I have seen the criticisms in all shapes and sizes. I have seen teams shine on projects. I have seen IT departments make a substantial impact on organizations. I have seen individual contributors become effective leaders.

As you move forward in your career, I hope this book is useful in providing context and guidance to the many challenges you will face. I have written it for those of you that read a book cover to cover and those of you that scan the table of contents and go to a specific topic.

Whether you are someone who wants to lead IT someday, have just started out as a new IT leader, or have been leading IT for years, I hope you will find the contents helpful.

Let's get started.

Part 1

Foundations

CHAPTER 1

FOUNDATIONS OVERVIEW

Architects create long-lasting buildings built on sound foundations. The best athletes are excellent at all the basic skills. A sound foundation is necessary for long-lasting excellence. Our leadership of the Information Technology department depends on us having foundational skills and concepts.

This part of the book presents basic concepts I will build on in the rest of the book.

Most of the concepts rely on an understanding of topics outside the IT world. You will note some recommendations for searches and additional reading throughout the book. These can give you additional background on these topics.

Chapter 2

Square Root Of Change

Back in the early 1990s, I was working in IT at a multi-billion dollar manufacturing company. Ours was a small part of IT, separate from the main IT organization. Responsible for about 2000 employees in our area, we had implemented several large projects over a two-year span; all bringing changes to the employees. These were cool projects. We replaced the email system. We changed everyone's username to match the corporate standard. We introduced a new (at the time) distributed computing model. I was a young IT acolyte, and I thought all change was good. Why were people so grumpy?

Sigh. I was so naïve.

This experience got me thinking about change and the journey from start to finish. There is a lot written about change management and I won't rehash that here other than to reinforce the primary point: If we don't pay attention to the change management process — intentionally think about how we will implement the change — we will make the project harder than it needs to be and make it harder for the business to see the expected benefits.

Riding the bus home after work one spring day, I was doodling in my notebook. While thinking about the projects we had implemented and the difficult changes the employees had gone through — a shape popped out to me.

The Square Root of Change.

Yes, yes, it is a little cheesy, but stay with me here. I think it helps us approach change in any project by understanding what we can control, what we can't control, and how people consider change.

Obviously, the name gives it all away, but let's walk through it anyway. One more thing, this is most applicable when the change involves people. If we are improving something behind the scenes, like increasing the speed of the internet connection into a building, this typically doesn't apply.

Square Root of Change

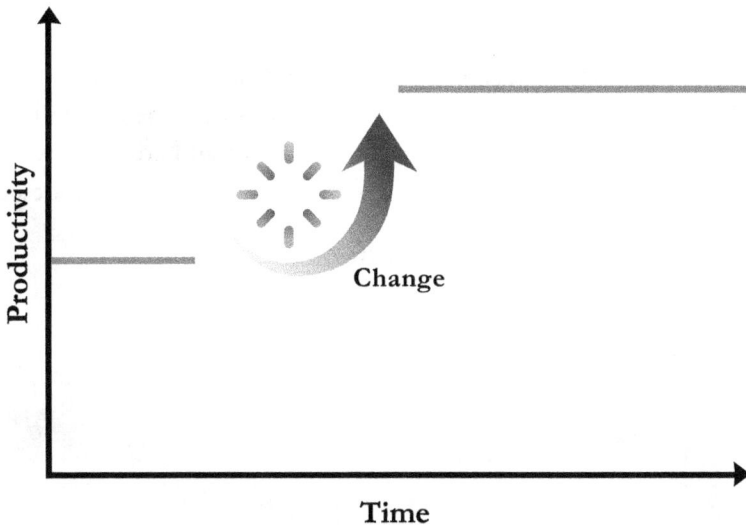

Let's start with the left axis. We implement change in order to make something better. A change could be to improve productivity, improve security, or reduce waste. A change could be to move from a dying application to one better supported by the vendor. We might implement a change to improve our expense situation.

So, the left axis shows what we are improving. I will use productivity for now. The concept applies regardless of what we are improving.

Improving productivity means that we start at a certain level and will end up at a better level.

Take a look at the first illustration to see what I mean.

Great, we are going to make things better. However, there is a catch. It is never a straight line from today's status to tomorrow's improvement. There is always a dip. Said another way, there will always be a drop in productivity (or whatever we are trying to improve) as we implement the change.

I think it helps us approach change in any project by understanding what we can control, what we can't control, and how people consider change.

Why is this?

People.

Now, this isn't because people are stupid or difficult. It isn't because people are resistant to change. It is because, even with the simplest change, people need to learn a new way of doing things and adjust how they do their job. When we add this drop in, we can see our square root shape.

Square Root of Change

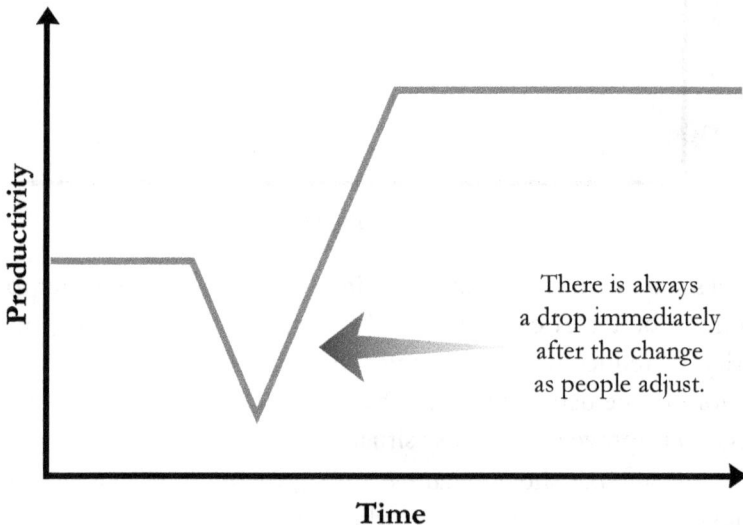

There is always a drop immediately after the change as people adjust.

Let's look in more detail at the dip. The depth of the dip is the severity of the drop in productivity. For example, if productivity is number of orders entered per day, we might expect a five or ten percent drop for a short time. The specifics, of course, depend on the change and what is being measured.

At some point, we hit the bottom. This is the lowest point of our productivity dip. It's uphill from here. We are still below the original productivity level, so we are still worse off than before we started. But our measurements show we are getting better.

Some more time passes, and we are now back to the same point we started from. The same productivity level as when we started. The duration of the change is the time between the change and this point. Depending on the change, the duration can be hours, days, weeks, or even months.

The last illustration illustrates the severity and duration.

Square Root of Change

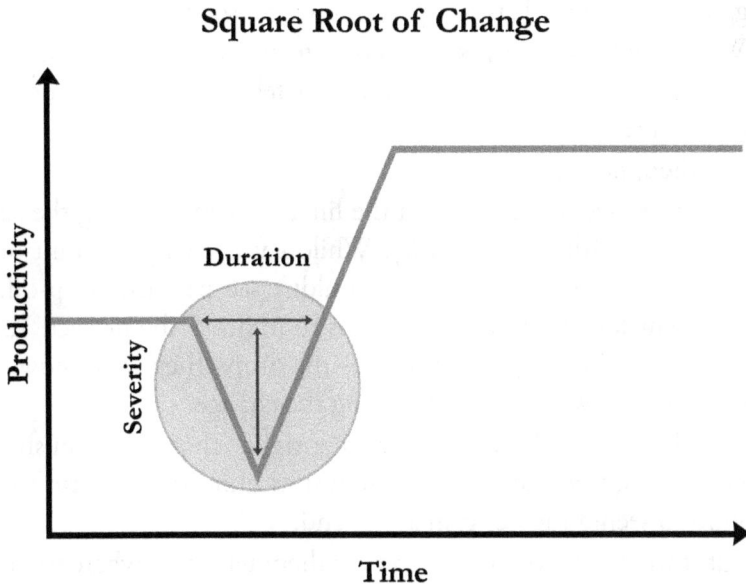

The following two points are true for any IT change involving people:

- Severity: There will be a temporary drop in what we are trying to improve.
- Duration: It will take time to get back to where we started, and only after that will we see our improvements.

The good news is that we have control over the duration and severity of the drop. This model provides a way to evaluate techniques we might use to help the change.

The specific things we do will usually impact duration or severity, but sometimes we get lucky and it benefits both. For example, training, data migration, documentation, appropriate testing, and good planning can reduce both.

Of course, clear and frequent communication about the change is also a must. A single email is rarely sufficient. People get too many emails these days, and emails from IT rarely get top priority in their inbox.

Now what about those grumpy people? People grumpy with change. Well, some people are always grumpy, can't change that. But some really struggle with change. It is just part of their personality.

When I talked with people, trying to make them understand how awesome a particular change would be, I felt like they were not seeing the big picture.

But then, neither was I.

They were seeing the drop in the line. They were seeing the severity of the change with perfect clarity. While I was trying to point out the eventual higher productivity, they couldn't see past the drop-off. And I was too clueless to use their opinions to improve the project. You see, they were pointing out the terrain for the drop. They were showing me the problems we will encounter during the change.

It took me a while to see they were right. Those of us pushing for change don't always see that. We are just as blind to their truth as they are blind to seeing the net gain at the end.

But if we listen closely, we can hear them telling us where to do extra training. Where to do some extra data cleanup. Where to slip in a few pop-up windows with transition help. Where to go faster or slower. They give us a map to navigate the change. Use it.

Find the loud, grumpy non-IT people and make sure you understand where they are coming from. Take the time to help them understand the change and the project will be better. If they add their voice to those advocating for the change, it only helps.

The Square Root of Change is a model for thinking about the inevitable problem with change. It is a model to mitigate the temporary drop in productivity (or whatever is being improved). It can help us navigate the duration and severity of the transition.

And keep us from being clueless like I was.

CHAPTER 3

FOCUS & FINISH

I stared at the list of requests the team was working on. Seven people, ninety-three active requests. Over ten active requests for each person. The team was working hard, but it felt like we weren't making progress. Requests were not getting completed, and it felt like we were the bottleneck. Sure, some active requests were waiting for people outside of IT to test or provide requirements. Most, however, were waiting for our team to work on them. We felt like we were spinning our wheels, not making any progress on the active requests. And the pile of waiting projects kept getting bigger and bigger, like a rising flood.

The IT department's to-do list is always longer than its capacity to complete those tasks. This is intentional. A properly managed company will not have excess capacity in its service groups like Finance, HR, or IT. I have yet to discover a company that does not have an IT backlog.

Getting that work done is a challenge. There is always pressure to do more. Those with requests in the backlog will keep pushing to get their requests completed. We complicate this by having too many projects or tasks active at the same time. We are always multitasking, trying to keep all the juggling balls up in the air.

All too often, we fail.

The answer is to have fewer tasks active at a time and make sure that they get completed before starting something new. Let's start with the real problem: multi-tasking.

Multitasking is a Myth

Multi-tasking is a myth. Scientific and business research has shown repeatedly that we can't multitask, we can only multi-switch. Each time we make a switch, it takes our brain a bit to switch back and forth. The bigger the mental challenge, the longer it takes to make the switch. We can switch between watching a show and browsing the internet if we aren't thinking deeply on either task. Switching between work tasks is harder because it takes more effort to transition.

Multitasking is a myth

Think about a triathlon: transitioning from swimming to biking is hard, and it takes a mile or two to complete the transition and get into the groove. The transition from biking to running has the same problem.

In the 24 Hours of La Mans car race, cars pull into the pits, swap drivers and take off again. While it only takes a few seconds to change the drivers, the time that matters is the time from driving at full speed until the car is back up to full speed. Our brain works the same way. Switching between tasks is not a sudden change, like changing gears, it is instead like changing drivers. The time we spend shifting from one task to another adds up, making us less efficient. It takes longer to get back to full speed than it does to swap drivers.

When we transition from one mental task to another, we have the same problem. No two problems are exactly alike, and our brain will take time to make the switch. This transition time is not productive and is a waste of time. For example, we waste time putting one task away and getting the new task out and trying to remember where we left off. I'll list some other examples in a bit.

This is time that we are not making progress on the tasks. If we reduce the number of transitions, we have more productive time.

The following diagram shows what is happening. In the first example, we only transition after we have completed a task. Three tasks, two transitions.

In the second example, we start all three tasks and try to spend a bit of time on each and we move them together towards completion. As you can see, we waste more time in transitions. All three tasks take longer to complete than if we had completed them one at a time.

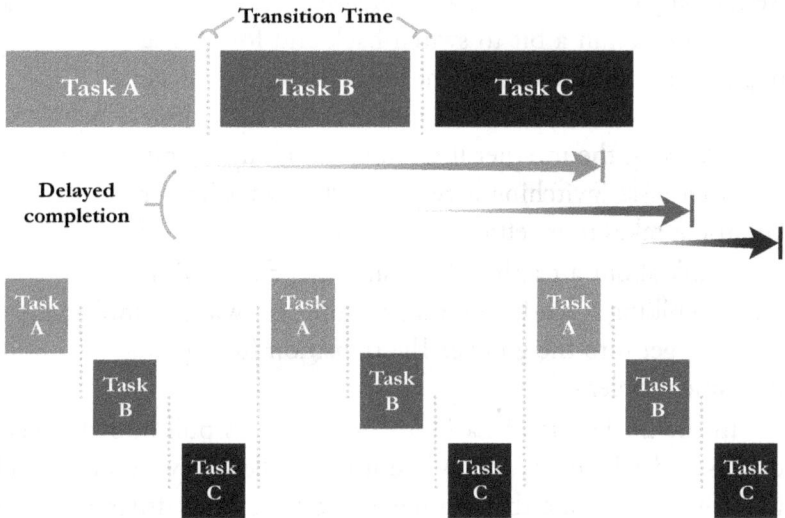

The illustration shows what happens when we try to switch between tasks. The more we switch between tasks, the more transitions we have and the longer it takes to complete the tasks.

The transition time in the illustration represents the delays that get introduced. Some of those delays are:

- Our mental transition time. It takes time to load the new task into our head. We need to remember what was happening with all the parts of the task. Did I remember to send that email? Did I finish the requirements? Where was I on writing the test plan? Where was I in the code?

- Scheduling delays. We get something ready and then we schedule a meeting. People's calendars are busy, so the meeting is a few days out. So we set it aside and go work on something else. When it comes time for the meeting, we have to reload all the thinking around the requirements back into our brains. Get the meeting on people's calendars first so you finish the requirements just in time for the meeting. Perhaps even walking through the requirements with them instead of having them read it before.

- Forgetting. This is especially true for smaller tasks. We all get them: hallway conversations, quick emails, actions from meetings. It is hard to remember everything and hard to get everything completely captured on a To-Do list.

We need to focus on a few tasks and complete them before starting new ones.

Completing the Task

What does "finished" mean? What is "complete"? We have a task in front of us and we need to take it to completion. If we need to gather requirements, we schedule a meeting, click Send, and we move on. We push a new version of an application out into production, make sure it works, and we move on. We stand up a new server, convert people over, and we move on.

We may have moved on to other tasks, but we didn't really finish. Did we put the latest version of code into our source code repository with all the right labeling and documentation? Do we need to prepare for the meeting? Did we remove the two old applications that got replaced by a new application? Did we verify no one is using the old server any longer and shut it down?

For each of our tasks, we need to define what "finished" means. We have a nice list at the start of the project containing all the loose ends we need to remember to clean up. Chances are, some of those things don't get done because the next project needs to start and is more important. We have all seen projects where this finishing work does not get done.

If we own a horse, we must put the saddle and other tack away and properly cool down and clean the horse. While you might convince yourself that not doing it *this one time* might be OK, ignoring these finishing tasks will cause problems in the long run.

If we don't finish the tasks completely, we will pay a price. Maybe not on each task, but eventually. Whether it be the accumulation of technical debt (chapter 6) or information that gets lost over time, the organization is worse off because we didn't truly finish.

We need to finish the tasks we start.

Focus & Finish

To deal with the twin problems of the multitasking myth and the need to complete all the work, I would like to introduce a simple concept that has served me well: Focus & Finish.

Focus on the most important tasks. Completely finish the project before moving on to the next one.

We must focus on the most important tasks. Focus on the task that is active right now. Focus on the highest priority project. We must have only a few tasks active.

Finish the project. We must completely finish the project before moving on to the next one.

Think of this as more of an approach than a hard and fast rule. It is also something that is very hard to do, for reasons I will cover in a moment. I have used this concept for the last ten years and it is still a constant battle for me.

This isn't easy to do. Life and work will conspire to force us off the path. Let's look at some specific situations that make it hard to Focus & Finish. I've also included some antidotes to each situation.

1. Waiting for something.

Tasks and projects often have times when we are waiting for someone else to do something and get back to us. When this happens, we need something else to work on. That new task then hits a "need something from someone" point and it gets set aside. Now we have two active tasks waiting for someone else to get back to us. So we start a third one, and so on.

While this is a legitimate reason for having several tasks open at a time, we need to be careful. Deadlines and expectations can offer a clue on the multi-car pileup that will happen when several of those tasks come back to us all at once. Now we are the bottleneck again.

Antidotes:

- Don't send emails to users telling them that something is ready and then wait for days or weeks for a response. Have a working meeting to go through it. Pick up the phone and call them.
- Put deadlines on every request for testing.
- Have regular progress meetings to keep the users up to speed.
- Don't wait until something is complete to schedule a review meeting. People's calendars are typically full enough that it is difficult to schedule a meeting on that day. Scheduling the meeting out into the future just introduces delays. If we schedule the meeting on the day we will finish, we can avoid that delay. Risky, but we should be able to know when we get inside the one-week window.
- Just stop by the person's desk to give them an update or run a critical design point by them.

2. Desire to Help.

The stronger the service mentality we have, the more likely we are going to fall into this trap. Someone calls us on the phone or sends us a text or email asking for something. We pick up three tasks from conversation just going to and from the bathroom. Wanting to help, we agree to get right on it. This adds to whatever number of tasks we had open.

Antidotes:

- Make sure that the company knows we work off a priority list. The more the company knows this, the easier it is for our team to say "I'll put it on the list."

- Implement a more formal method for submitting requests. Build the discipline in our teams to hold users to it.

3. External forces.

There are forces outside our control that occasionally require we put aside our current task. I have had situations where several of them have hit at the same time. The deadlines make it worse, as it doesn't seem possible to do them one at a time.

Sometimes they are from the business. We need to address an urgent Customer problem that comes in. An audit finding has to be closed in thirty days. A lucrative partnership opportunity pops up that requires system changes.

Sometimes they have technical origins. A Windows update breaks a Customer application. A cloud service rolls out an update that has a user interface change that causes a bunch of questions from our user population. We have all experienced them and there isn't much we can do other than try to prevent them. It might be in the best interest of the business to have IT drop what we are doing and take care of them.

Antidotes:

- We can't prevent these from happening. When they do, we must communicate with all involved. We will never get everyone to be happy about it, but we should strive to have everyone understand it.
- In rare circumstances, we might shuffle tasks to keep the original tasks moving. This is easier with a larger team. Just remember that something, hopefully the lowest priority task, will fall off our plates and not get completed.

4. Limited People with needed skills.

The individuals on our team have strengths and knowledge. For any request, there will be a set of people that can handle it, sometimes one person, sometimes sever-

There will always be a bottleneck somewhere in our department. If not, we are over-staffed.

al. If there are more requests requiring a set of skills than people that are good in that area, there is a bottleneck.

For example, if several business projects with heavy reporting requirements hit at one time, the load falls on a few people. Developers can also be a bottleneck.

In fact, there will always be a bottleneck somewhere in our department. If not, we are over-staffed. We need to be aware of the bottleneck and manage the surrounding work.

Antidotes:

- If we understand the trend of requests, we can increase skills in the area where bottlenecks happen.
- Remove the non-bottleneck tasks from individuals that are the bottleneck. In our example above, removing all non-reporting work will allow them to focus on the bottlenecked requests.
- If the surge is big enough, consider using outside resources.

5. *"IT is too slow, let's focus on small things that they can get done quickly."*
How many times have we heard the organization say this? The more there is a priority list driving our activities, the more this one shows up. People who can't get their projects to the top of the list try to figure out minor tasks they hope will slip through the cracks in the priority list. *"It will only take a few minutes, right?"* Our team, to be helpful, tries to work them in. Before we know it, there are too many active tasks.

Also keep in mind that there are very few actual minor requests. It isn't just the five minutes to change the value in the source code; it is also the code management, IT testing, business testing, releasing, etc.

Antidotes:

- Keep the priority conversation focused on the higher priority tasks. Continue to show how they tie into the larger organizational priorities.
- Complete requests. This seems like an obvious one, but if we aren't showing completion of requests, it will feel like IT isn't accomplishing anything.

- Size the request properly. Avoid tasks that take months.
- Use an agile approach. Often the initial request contains the most benefit. We can break the add-on tasks out into a separate request. The requesters won't like it, but it allows them to get the primary benefit faster and we can move on to the next request sooner.

6. Zombie Projects.

We all know these. Projects that just drag on and on and on and on. People change, priorities change, requirements change. Tasks that were urgent for one person one month becomes much lower priority when that person moves on or has more important tasks. Delays and project resets contribute to the problem. People assigned to these zombie projects get a haunted look in their eyes as they shamble back and forth to the coffee machine. We can try to move the project back to the inactive list during the delays, but then it will pop up again and again.

I want to make a special shout out to the biggest zombie creator of all: scope creep. The team continues to add requirements and doesn't prioritize them. There is a fear by the users that, if we don't add the new requirements now, they will never get added.

There is only one way to kill a zombie. Be ruthless in killing zombie projects. Also, it is helpful if we have taken sword lessons.

sunk cost porblem

Antidotes:

- Prioritize requirements. Use the "black-line" model for prioritization: Prioritize the requirements and insert a black line in the middle. If a requirement above the line takes longer, the go live date slips. If a requirement below the line takes longer, it gets dropped from the release.
- Quantify the organizational impact of delays. If there is value in the work ready to go, what is the daily cost for not putting it into production?
- Learn about the sunk cost problem and how to avoid it.

7. Sometimes our teams need a mental break.

Upgrading a major system typically takes a long time. It is hard to stay 100% focused on the same project for months. The team needs a break once in a while. I'm a fan of the mental floss idea: a minor task, different from the larger task, can provide us with a mental break. A small task we can finish and feel good about. A small task that uses a different part of our brain. Just like dental floss cleans out the junk that accumulates between our teeth, mental floss can clean out our brain of the junk that accumulates during a large project. For example, I give the team a brief window after an ERP upgrade to do nothing but small change requests to build up that sense of accomplishment again. Sometimes this needs to happen during the project to recharge their batteries.

Antidotes:

- Only do this when it allows your team to refresh on large projects.
- Only schedule this between other tasks. Continue to keep the number of active tasks small.
- There is obviously a conflict between this one and #5. Using your judgment is the only way around it.

8. Changing Priorities.

This one is tough. If our organization doesn't have a good prioritization process, we may end up switching as one project falls out of favor and another becomes the project du jour.

Antidotes:

- Avoid putting projects on hold for priority reasons. Kill the project, if you must. Or try to get a partial solution into production.
- If the organization doesn't have clear priorities, turn the IT prioritization conversation into a business priority conversation. If we keep asking why one request is more important that another, the conversation will eventually get to what is important to the business.

9. Customer Needs.

When a Customer request comes in that requires IT help, it is typically best to stop the other work and take care of it. Not much we can do about this one. Customers come first. Perhaps if they are regular requests, we can put a process in place to do them quickly and accurately, but I haven't had too many situations like that. They are usually unique and require immediate attention. (I'm talking about real Customers, not those fake internal ones. I'll get to that soon.)

Antidotes:

- There isn't much to do to prevent these. In fact, it is to the organization's benefit to handle Customer requests quickly while effectively managing the disruption of internal projects.

Focus & Finish Is Worth the Effort

As I mentioned, Focus & Finish is an approach, not a set of rules to follow. It requires constant diligence. Just when you think you have it under control, you will find the number of active tasks getting bigger.

As a leader, we can provide our team with the processes, prioritization, and, sometimes, the external excuse to prevent too many active tasks at a time. Sometimes our employees appreciate being able to tell others, *"My boss told me I have to wait to start your project."*

Regular conversations about what "complete" means can help the Finish part. Point out when prior tasks are not being completed properly or we haven't cleaned up the technical debt. Allow your team to have that time at the end of the project to finish completely, without pushing the last tasks off the table like a cat with a water glass. We need to create the space for them to finish.

Focus & Finish will help us and our teams to finish more work. Keep the number of active projects small (FOCUS!) and make sure they are complete before moving on (FINISH!).

CHAPTER 4

RISK MANAGEMENT

Risk assessment and risk management are important tools in our toolbox. We make decisions every day that balance the risks of different situations.

In this chapter, I will provide risk assessment background and talk about how it applies to IT. If you already understand likelihood, severity, and detectability, skip to the last section.

During my time working outside of IT, I worked for a medical device company as a project manager. Safety is critical for medical devices. To make sure a medical device is safe, each design project had both a Hazard Analysis (HA) and a Failure Modes Effect Analysis (FMEA). Medical device companies integrate the Risk Management processes into the design process.

The HA treats the design as a "solid box" — that is, we don't know how it works inside. To create a HA, we list the ways the device can hurt the patient or operator, do a risk assessment on that list, and then mitigate the unacceptable risks.

The FMEA treats the design as a "glass box" — we know the details of the design. We go through each part of the design and list the ways each part of the design can fail. Like the HA, we do a risk assessment on each failure and mitigate the unacceptable risks.

HAs and FMEAs are formal processes with lots of rules. We use them on medical, aerospace, defense, and other projects where failure can cause significant personal harm. These industries have developed these techniques to understand and reduce risks.

We can use the concept of risk management in our IT work to make decisions, schedule projects, and manage people. We may already have a section in our projects where we list the risks. Risk Management techniques will let us use that list more effectively.

We will benefit the most from the informal use of risk assessment, but let's take a moment to go over the formal method first to set our foundation.

The three major components of risk assessment are (1) *Likelihood*: What are the chances the event will happen? (2) *Severity*: How bad it is if the event happens? (3) *Detectability*: How easy is it to notice the event is happening?

In formal risk assessment, these three components are assigned numbers, with higher numbers for worse situations. These numbers get a lot of discussion in the formal process, but I won't go into that detail here. We will use "1" to represent a low value, "3" as a medium value, and "5" as a high value. Don't worry about the numbers, the math is simple and we only use them in formal risk assessment. Note also that the terminology may be different in different industries — focus on the concepts, not the words.

Likelihood

Risk assessments capture unwanted events that might happen. If there is absolutely no chance something will happen, it doesn't go on the list. If there is a 100% chance it will happen, then it belongs in the project plan, not the risk assessment. With these edge cases eliminated, it leaves us with unwanted events that have some possibility of occurring.

Think of each event in the risk assessment as a column on a spreadsheet. The first row to worry about is Likelihood. This shows how probable it is that this event will happen.

The simplest way to capture this information is Low, Medium, or High. An event that isn't likely to happen gets a "1" rating. We put a "5" on an event that will probably happen. We give a "3" to things in between.

So imagine a risk for a mythical medical device. We might have the following risk events and likelihood:

	Minor Event	Medium Event	Major Event
Likelihood	1	3	5
Severity			
Detectability			
Risk Factor			
Notes			

Severity

Severity covers the impact of the event if it happens. In the medical device world, the high severity is when the device injures or kills someone or gives a wrong reading or diagnosis. An example of a low severity is when the operator navigates to a wrong screen and has to go back and select the correct screen.

Severity is the answer to the question: What's the worst thing that can happen?

Keep in mind that there may be indirect effects from a risk. For example, when the first failure causes a subsequent failure. In the medical device world, think of the initial risk of tripping over the power cord that causes a secondary risk of pulling something out of the patient.

A quick aside: while the above examples are obvious, assigning numbers is more of a judgment call than a set of hard and fast rules. My suggestion is don't worry about the specifics of setting the numbers. Do a quick pass with Low, Medium, High and put the numbers in. If in doubt, pick the worst case.

Updating the severity row, we get the following table:

	Minor Event	Medium Event	Major Event
Likelihood	1	3	5
Severity	1	3	5
Detectability			
Risk Factor			
Notes			

Detectability

Sometimes we notice when an unwanted event happens, sometimes we don't. Detectability captures that in our table. Note that detectability is of the event itself, not the results of the event. It is the ability to detect the failure itself, not the injuries that may happen from the failure.

In the IT world, something going wrong with our manufacturing lead time calculations might be an example of a hard to detect event. We trust the output, and if the error is subtle, we might not notice a failure. In contrast, a problem with log file cleanup is easy to detect with disk space monitoring.

Applying the detectability numbers brings us this table:

	Minor Event	Medium Event	Major Event
Likelihood	1	3	5
Severity	1	3	5
Detectability	1	3	5
Risk Factor			
Notes			

We have completed our very short risk assessment with numbers for Likelihood, Severity, and Detectability. A real medical device might have hundreds of events listed.

Risk Factor

How do we go from the risk assessment to risk management? In formal risk management, we multiply the three component numbers to get the Risk Factor. If the Risk Factor is too high, we need to mitigate, that is, reduce, the risk.

Formal risk assessment requires that we define a risk threshold number and compare the risk factors against it. The specific risk threshold number isn't important here, so let's just say 75. If the risk factor is above the threshold, we must mitigate the risk. We reduce the risk factor by one of three things: (1) making it less likely to happen, (2) making it less severe, or (3) making it easier to detect.

Creating mitigations for high-risk events makes the design better, and makes it less likely that a particular event will cause a problem. For example, in our table, if we update the design to change the major event detectability from a "5" to a "1", the risk factor reduces to 25, which is below our threshold to mitigate.

	Minor Event	Medium Event	Major Event
Likelihood	1	3	5
Severity	1	3	5
Detectability	1	3	5
Risk Factor	1	27	125
Notes	No Mitigation Needed	No Mitigation needed	Mitigation needed

To review, the following steps comprise the formal risk assessment:

1. List the risk events that may occur.
2. Determine the Likelihood, Severity, and Detectability for each event and assign a number value.
3. For each risk event, multiply the three components numbers together to get the Risk Factor.
4. Set a Risk Factor threshold and mitigate all risks with a higher Risk Factor.
5. Repeat until all Risk Factors are below our threshold.

Practice helps. Try it out on a small IT change that has some risk. List all the things that can go wrong. Assign numbers for likelihood, severity, and detectability. Multiply them together to get the risk factor. Take the highest Risk Factor numbers and implement mitigations. Repeat until we have reached the point of diminishing returns.

How To Use Risk Assessment in IT

Now that we have some exposure to the formal method of risk assessment and mitigation, let's look at it in the IT world. We will rarely use the formal method, so what does an informal method look like?

In informal risk management, we rarely use the table with all the numbers. We may list only a few risks as we need not be as complete as medical device design requires. We may only do a quick comparison of the risk components and see if it sets off our "need to mitigate" trigger.

Make the risk less likely to happen. Make the risk less severe if it happens. And make it easier to detect when the risk happens.

The key is to apply the three mitigation approaches to the worst risks. Make the risk less likely to happen. Make the risk less severe if it happens. And make it easier to detect when the risk happens.

Experience builds a sense of where the risks are on a project. Introducing new technology always has risks. A department that always changes requirements mid-project needs mitigation on scope creep. A vendor that starts releasing bug-filled versions should be mitigated right out of our organization. We should trust our instincts and think about how to mitigate the likelihood, severity, and detectability of these risks.

Let's look at some examples of how this might work:

- Improving the detectability can be straightforward for technical problems. Various monitors or reports can alert our teams to problems when they occur. In fact, "detect the problem before the user does" should be part of our basic strategy. Feed those alerts into the Help Desk system so they get attention right away, and we can solve problems before they affect users.

- Testing is the best tool for reducing the likelihood of a problem happening. Putting the system or process through real-world test scenarios is critical. Having a test environment identical to the production environment makes the testing more effective. End user testing brings a different view of the system than IT testing.

- The "Show Your Work" technique (chapter 23) is helpful in user testing and for improving detectability once the system is in production.

Besides project risk, we can use risk assessment to improve our decisions. Often, a decision is between two or three options. Consider the risks of each choice from a likelihood, severity, and detectability point of view. Is one choice less risky than the others? Or maybe one choice has a bigger single risk and becomes a better choice if we mitigate that risk.

We don't need to become an expert on risk assessment, we just need to know enough to apply the principles to our job.

Risk management is also important when proposing large projects. We need to show we have thought through the potential problems and have plans in place to mitigate the worst risks.

There are common risks on IT projects that we can preload into our risk assessment. Some of them are:

- Insufficient IT resources available
- Business resources unavailable when needed
- Development takes longer than expected
- Requirements change over time
- Incomplete Test Scenarios

We don't need to become an expert on risk assessment, we just need to know enough to apply the principles to our job. Likelihood, Severity, and Detectability. Mitigate to reduce risk. It is surprising how often this is a useful tool.

CHAPTER 5

PROACTIVITY IS OVERRATED

Today is tomorrow's yesterday. What happens today will affect the future, whether it is tomorrow, next week, next month, or next year. The future always arrives. These are all cliche ways of saying the same thing: We need to always think about the future. Everything we do today affects us, our team, and the company in the future.

How do we balance the needs of today with the needs of the future? The future is vague and impossible to predict with any accuracy. The pressures of today, such as *"We need to fix this immediately!"* often directly conflict with making tomorrow better. This makes it harder to be proactive.

We know that being proactive is better than being reactive. Anticipating the future and taking actions to deal with future events is the right approach. Reacting to events can make us appear slow. Being proactive and not reactive has been excellent advice for many years. Being proactive as an individual and an organization is a good thing. It is essential to try to see the likely future and prepare for it.

We need to be proactive where we can. We should look into the future and do our best to put our departments in the best place for what will probably happen.

Proactivity is important, and we should strive to do more of it. However, I believe that proactivity is overrated and insufficient. In this chapter, I will explain why I think getting better at reacting is necessary.

Being proactive is not enough

Being proactive means anticipating the future and taking actions appropriate for that future.

However, there are two major shifts in the world that make reactivity more important than we might expect: (1) everything is changing faster, and (2) people expect things to change faster. These two forces are making it harder to be proactive because predicting the future is getting harder. Proactivity can no longer be the exclusive goal.

> Proactivity is important, and we should strive to do more of it. However, I believe that proactivity is overrated and insufficient.

Some events are easy to predict. If our company has plans for growth, the IT department needs to put processes in place to handle a larger number of employees, computers, transactions, and so forth. We can predict that most of our licensed software will have newer versions in the next year. It is easy to be proactive for these events.

But not all events are this easy to predict. Let's look a little deeper at what we have to get right to live fully proactively.

First, we have to be smart. We have to predict everything that is going to happen. And we must predict *when* something will happen as well as the *magnitude*.

If we predict that our company will grow by fifty employees over the next year, but we end up onboarding one hundred employees in the next quarter, we didn't get it right. And we will have to react.

We have to predict that a Customer's requirements for a new product will require changes to our central system. Including predicting the specific changes.

We have to implement defenses against all possible cyber-attacks that might happen. We have to predict our company will get purchased. Being able to predict all these things correctly is not possible.

Another factor is that our predictions will be wrong. The easiest way to see this is to look at decisions made before we took the job. We wonder at a situation and asked ourselves, "Why did they decide to do it that way?" How many times have we criticized past decisions of ourselves or someone else? Former employees seem to be an unfortunate target for this type of criticism.

All the criticism that we level against the past will be leveled against us someday. We, and others, will look at our decisions in the rear-view mirror. Will we be happy with the decisions and actions we are taking today? Did we predict the future accurately?

How many times have we criticized past decisions of ourselves or someone else?

If seeing the future clearly is a strength of ours, we are lucky. Our life will be easier. But I know I am not that smart.

We should try to be proactive where we can, but know that the world is changing and forcing our organizations to react more of the time. We can't completely rely on being proactive. We must get better at reacting.

But how?

Can we get better at reacting? Can we see events and identify and execute a solution quicker than last year? The answer, of course, is yes. We can get better at reacting.

I propose that *Speed* and *Flexibility* are the two critical attributes of our organization that support this.

If our department is fast at identifying when events occur, we can start our reaction faster. If our department is flexible, we can come up with a better solution. If we are fast and flexible, we can implement the solution quickly and correctly.

In the next two sections, I will dive into Speed and Flexibility in more detail. But first, I want to introduce a concept that helps us understand the importance of reacting.

The OODA Loop

There is a concept originally developed by the military called the OODA Loop. The acronym stands for Observe, Orient, Decide, Act. The word "loop" implies we do this continually.

Developed in the 1950s as a way to understand how to win battles, it has since been applied to other fields. This section will discuss how it applies to the IT field. Let's go through the individual words first.

OODA Loop

Observe

Observe refers to gathering data and information about the current situation. This is not a onetime data gathering exercise, but is a constant stream coming into the decision makers. In IT, this can be metrics, business needs, change requests, industry news, financial reports, etc. This data and information covers the behaviors of IT, the business, and the outside world. It can come to us in emails, magazines, reports, seminars, peer group meetings, and other methods.

It is important that the data stream captures both current and potential future states. How is our team performing? How is the company performing? What is happening today in the industry? What technology trends are taking off? Which trends are fading away?

Our data stream needs to be intentional. We need to decide what information, or information sources, we want to be coming at us regularly. And we need to make time to take it in. We won't be able to spend as much time on this as we would like, so we need to prioritize the data and information.

Our data stream will have informal information as well. For example, conversations with our staff to maintain a good understanding of how each person is doing. I try to have monthly one-on-one meetings where we discuss, even briefly, the larger picture of how they are doing at work. Are they enjoying their job? Do they have everything they need to be successful? This is only one minor example.

Having a rich pipeline of data and information coming in gives us the raw material for the next step.

Orient

While all the steps in the OODA loop are important, getting oriented in all the data and information is where most of our mistakes occur. It is hard to interpret everything properly in the information stream.

I came across a fun little game where one person finds an obscure place on land in a digital map, zooms way in, and hands it to another person. The second person's goal is to figure out where they are on the planet with a minimum amount of zooming out. A person wins by guessing their location on the planet and zooming out the least.

This game forces the players to orient themselves on the planet based on a limited amount of information. The better we use the clues the mapping software provides, the better we do.

The same is true for IT. The better we understand where our department and the company stand in the larger picture, the better oriented we are.

The challenge is that this isn't a simple physical location problem. We have an almost infinite number of ways to define where our departments are in the world. How well are our help desk and change request processes working? What is the current state of each person on our staff? How old is the technology we depend on, and how well are we using it? What upgrade projects should we do in the next year? What business challenges are happening today and what IT resources will they need?

We cannot come to a perfectly clear understanding of these things. We will never be perfectly oriented. We can only do our best to have a constantly updated picture of where things stand today.

But today is not enough. Our observations must help us orient to potential future situations. This is even harder than being well oriented to the current situation. We should not underestimate the value of forward-looking information in our stream.

Decide

The next step in the OODA loop is Decide. We have observations coming in constantly as we keep ourself and our department oriented in the world. We have a sense of where things are in the moment and have an idea of possible futures. This step covers the decisions we make and the actions we take. A simple way to think of it is "deciding what to do next."

These decisions will be both small and large, and we make them constantly. When we drive a car, we look at the immediate, local situation such as where we are in the lane and what vehicles are around us. We are also looking at the larger picture, such as getting into the correct lane to make a turn up ahead, or how much longer before we need to refuel the car.

Our IT decisions will be the same. Small, local changes like reminding staff of a minor change in the help desk process. Or larger ones like figuring out the best time to invest in a major new system.

We make these decisions constantly. We rarely have the luxury of taking time to do lots of research before making them. The better the Observe and Orient processes are, the easier it will be to Decide.

Act

After we decide, we need to act on it. We need to implement the decision and bring it to reality. A decision without an action is like deciding where we will go on vacation but never scheduling the time, never getting to our destination, and never taking that bungee jump off a cliff.

A decision with no action is not a decision. To be fair, sometimes we may decide what we will do in a potential future situation. *When Alex retires, I will move Marie into that position.* But if we don't take action or can delay the action until the future, we haven't really decided. This can work in our favor. They are *tentative decisions* and they are plans for potential future situations. Since we can always change them before we act, they aren't decisions yet.

Taking action on a decision means changing the behavior of people or systems. If there is no change, there has been no action, and therefore no decision.

We have more control over our own staff than we have over the situation outside the department or the organization. All our decisions will be about ourself, the department, and the company. When we take action, we should be able to see the results in our observations.

Looping

The four parts of the OODA loop, Observe, Orient, Decide, and Act are not discrete steps in a process that happens linearly. They are four processes that are happening each day. Four processes that are tightly interconnected. The article on the latest malware techniques that we read last week will influence today's decisions. A webinar we attend today may change our mind about how we should organize our help desk.

Understanding the four parts can be very useful to keeping everything straight in our minds. How are we doing on each part? How much time do we spend updating our orientation? Are our decisions turning into actions that change what we are observing?

Most non-military uses of the OODA loop focus on winning against competition. I would like to suggest that our best use of the OODA loop concept is to improve our *Speed* and *Flexibility*. By being fast to address situations, our IT department can better help our company meet its goals.

Speed

The speed of our organization matters. Customers always want things faster. Fast online shipping, mass customization, and other business innovations have raised Customer expectations.

The world is also changing extremely quickly. By any measure we look at, change is happening faster in technical, social, and

The ability of our company to respond quickly to changes and opportunities will determine its success.

economic areas. How well is our company dealing with change? How well is our IT department dealing with change?

The ability of our company to respond quickly to changes and opportunities will determine its success. If our company is slow, it needs to be very smart to get it right on the first try because competition won't give us a second chance. When competition disrupts our industry, we have to respond quickly or perish.

Thirty years ago, when I worked at a large company, a new CEO came in and was making the small group rounds. He said something that has stuck with me ever since: "*If we are faster than our competition; we don't need to be smarter.*" If our companies can try-fail-try-succeed faster than the competition can do a single try, we have a better chance of winning in the marketplace.

Speed is an accelerant for the sparks of brilliance. The faster our department, the better we can take advantage of the sparks of brilliance our teams produce.

The speed of the IT department is fundamental to the speed of the organization. Since many business changes require IT work to implement, a faster IT department will help the company change faster.

A faster development team will allow more cycles of an agile development process, putting new functionality in the hands of the users faster.

A faster Help Desk will return employees to working normally sooner, reducing downtime on a person-by-person basis.

A faster IT department will react to business changes faster, which may help win future business.

Here is a story that shows the benefits of speed.

The COVID-19 pandemic disrupted everyone's supply chain. Early on, Customers from the medical market sent emails wanting to know the impact of the virus on our product delivery. The manual process we had in place wouldn't scale. Hundreds of suppliers, many providing unique parts, combined with the unique nature of each company's COVID-19 response, made this a challenge.

Because of speed built into in our technology base (an existing data warehouse) and the speed of an IT employee, we created a generic solution that took a list of Customers and created the list of suppliers in very short order. The Supply Chain folks mapped this against the supplier COVID-19 status data we were collecting, allowing them to respond to the many Customer queries with a simple lookup that provided detailed supplier status from a single Customer ID.

Because we had the data warehouse in place and could quickly create this tool, we reacted quickly to Customer requests as they came in. Speed in developing the tool allowed our company to better react to the quickly changing situation.

While this solution isn't particularly unique or brilliant, the IT department's ability to create such a tool quickly helped the business respond to the situation, and the Customers.

How Can We Get Faster?

This is the tough question. There are two kinds of speed to look at: the speed of the individuals, and the speed of our processes.

Individuals work at the pace they work at. We know that some people are faster than others. This speed is part of who the person is and can't dramatically change.

However, speed by itself isn't the entire story. Quality of work comes into play also. At a medical device company, there was a device that had two major circuit boards with custom firmware on each. One engineer had their design done quickly and a test build done months before the other. But the fast design had problems, and we needed many changes to the board and software. Each iteration seemed to have problems. The "slow" engineer ended up completing her board first because there was only one round of very minor changes after the first design round.

Similarly, I have had Help Desk staff who are fast responding to problems, but didn't seem to have great luck fixing the problem on the first attempt. Multiple attempts meant they took longer than others to resolve the employee's problem.

So when evaluating our teams, we must pay attention not only to the time to get a first try complete. We must pay attention to how long it takes them to get done, meaning complete and correct, and not just how fast they respond.

When we look at our IT department, understanding speed gets more complicated. Knowledge of the company and health of our IT processes are the major factors here.

Let's look at knowledge of the company first. One point I will make in this book is that we, as IT leaders, have a major responsibility to understand the organization. This does not mean that we are the only one in the IT department that should know this. Some level of awareness of the organization, its major pieces, and the current drivers for each area is necessary for understanding the context of the requests that come in.

For example, our team's understanding of how order taking, planning, engineering, and the production floor interact, improves their response to requests. They can contribute to ideas and solutions because they know all the processes. When one of those groups asks for a change, our teams know who to talk to and the likely effects on the rest of the organization. When there is a problem, our teams know the downstream effects and the best resolution for the company, not just the group having the problem.

The next factor in improving the speed of our IT departments is the speed of our processes. I cover these in more detail elsewhere, but for now, let's look at a simplified view of IT processes: (1) fixing broken things, (2) implementing standard changes, and (3) implementing unique changes.

A standard change is one that happens frequently, but with different inputs. Examples include permission changes, folder access, some data changes, and employee

The fastest ticket to solve is the one that doesn't happen.

adds/terminations. Unique changes are those that apply to business processes and are never the same.

How do we speed up each of these processes? Here are some ideas:

- Improve the notes kept when solving problems so when the same problem comes up, Help Desk personnel can quickly find a prior solution. These knowledge bases are hard to keep updated and used effectively, but can be very helpful.

- The fastest ticket to solve is the one that doesn't happen. By spending some time preventing future tickets, our whole company wins. Having fewer help desk tickets makes more time for implementing changes. We can prevent tickets by fixing long-standing problems, training, documentation, and other techniques.

- Standard changes should have a process around each one. Spending a bit of time writing up the process and implementing a form for employees to fill out will allow our team to implement these standard changes quickly and correctly. Adding scripting will help speed and consistency.

- Unique changes require an overall process that emphasizes speed and quality. There will be a natural tendency to make the process more and more complicated in response to problems or improvement ideas. For example, a forty-page document on how to write requirements isn't very helpful if we aren't writing requirements when we should. Complicated processes are the opposite of speedy and rarely solve the quality problem.

Speed is critical to our department, but it isn't the only piece. The other side of the coin is flexibility, and I cover that next.

Flexibility

Another attribute to maximize in the IT department is flexibility. Closely related to speed, flexibility shows a *willingness* and *ability* to change. It is a fine line we have to walk. Standardization, protocols, processes, all make our department better able to meet the company's needs. But those same things can make our department less flexible.

How do we make our department more flexible?

- Create a culture of continuous improvement. A deep willingness and ability to change removes friction when implementing change. We need to reward this behavior when we see it.

- Avoid decisions that remove future options. Or be thoughtful about what options we remove. For example, if a new product has two different ways to interface and we won't be interfacing until a year after implementation, keep both interfaces available. Don't decide on one until the interface project starts and we have a better idea about the requirements.
- Enable and monitor Shadow IT in our company for ideas. I'll talk more about Shadow IT in chapter 24. For now, just consider this: Shadow IT happens because IT is too slow, too controlling, or too limiting. Understand the *why* behind Shadow IT and we can learn how to improve our department.

If we keep a trained eye on the long term (the business and technology) we should know what flexibility we need in the future. Some examples:

(1) The possibility of a home-grown application in a department getting replaced in the next few years, should drive some of our development decisions. Make the data and functionality similar to the likely future. For example, a company had a custom-built application for tracking sales opportunities but thought about buying a CRM. A small investigation into possibilities showed some common approaches. They changed the custom-built application to use those new concepts, making it easier to move to a purchased CRM down the road.

(2) Put an isolation layer between the application and a technology that will probably change down the road.

(3) Be careful about taking advantage of vendor specific lock-ins, especially at the infrastructure level. Sure, it is unlikely that we will change the underlying database vendor for our ERP system soon, but there is a

good chance that we will want to introduce a different development tool or language for applications.

(4) Be clear about where the original source data is, but be flexible about where and how to access that data. Being good at data sync allows us to separate the source of truth for a data set from the places that are updated or accessed. Keeping it only in one place limits future options. A good example of this is the list of active employees. The original source is probably in an HR system, but we will need the list in other places such as the ERP, a data warehouse, and various login accounts. Keeping a single list in the HR system and having all the other systems make calls back to the HR system sounds ideal, but in practice is not workable. Synchronizing the employee list to all the other places, making sure to only change it in the original location, can reduce complexity.

(5) When implementing a new wireless network, assume that the company will want it everywhere, not just in the places that exist today. For example, implementing an "everywhere wireless" instead of a "where needed wireless" provides additional flexibility on the manufacturing floor as we reduce the need to pull cables when the manufacturing floor changes.

Wrap Up

> *The best laid schemes of mice and men*
> *Go often askew,*
> *And leave us nothing but grief and pain,*
> *For promised joy!*
> — Robert Burns, *To A Mouse,* 1785

Mr. Burns didn't work in IT, but he speaks our truth. We need to be proactive, to plan for the future as best we can. But planning isn't enough. We will never predict the future correctly enough to avoid needing to react quickly and correctly. It is worth putting in the effort to improve our ability to react.

CHAPTER 6

TECHNICAL DEBT

The concept of Technical Debt has been around for decades. Originating in the software development area, Technical Debt describes the accumulation of "we should probably fix that" places in the code. As I will show, Technical Debt does not just apply to software, it applies to the entire IT world. Hardware, software, infrastructure, security, and applications all have their technical debt.

Technical Debt is a little like Schrodinger's Cat as it may or may not be there. Some technical debt is never a problem. Some of it blows up spectacularly. Some assumptions we make are fine. Others aren't.

Here are some examples:

- A small company doesn't put a Country field into their addresses because they have no plans to be international. Until five successful years later, when they do.
- In the 1970s, everyone knew they would replace their software by the year 2000, so two digits for the year were fine. Until it wasn't.
- A developer makes an undocumented assumption about the underlying operating system that eventually becomes false.

- The database developer writes code that only works with on-premise databases because there are no plans to move this critical database to the cloud. Until there are.

So how does this apply to other parts of IT? At some point, a decision gets made that predicts or assumes what will happen and that prediction or assumption is no longer valid. This miscalculation about the future is hard to avoid because pretty much every decision or action in IT is assuming a certain future:

- *"We won't need Wi-Fi in that location."*
- *"The chance of us needing 20 levels of approval is pretty slim."*
- *"There is no way that our ERP database will get even close to one terabyte."*

IT is about putting solutions in place to help the company. Everything IT delivers is used in the future. Given the speed of technological changes, is there any wonder some of our assumptions are wrong?

But there is some Technical Debt that we can avoid:

1. *"We'll finish that later."*
This often shows up at the end of the project. Standing up a new server, but not shutting down and disposing of the old one. Leaving a few users on the old system because it is too hard to move them to the new system. Not updating the documentation after a change. Leaving the implementation of a security feature for later and then realizing that it is too late to do so.

2. *"Let's see if this works."*
Did we clean up after a try/fail cycle when fixing a problem? There is a problem, so someone makes a change, thinking it will fix it. When that doesn't fix the problem, does the change get undone? Too many times, the answer is no. These little "wrong changes" sit out there like time bombs, causing future problems. For example, changing an Active

Directory setting for a user (which makes them different from everyone else) causes a future problem to display different symptoms. This makes it harder to solve that future problem.

3. *"Just patch it again."*

Imagine we are clearing brush in the woods and we get a cut on our arm. We put a bandage on it. We get another cut and put another bandage on it. Pretend we don't learn fast and we do this all day long. Soon we have dozens of these bandages all over our arm, limiting flexibility and making it hard to clear brush.

Or imagine a machine that gets fixed with bailing wire and twine for years. At some point, the fixes will overwhelm the proper functioning of the machine. When a problem occurs, do we take the time to make a more permanent fix or do we just add some more twine and keep going?

4. *"If it ain't broke, don't fix it."*

When the future of technology is speeding towards us like a grizzly on gallons of coffee, leaving things until tomorrow is sometimes necessary because of cost or other priorities, but it likely will cost us more time and money in the long run.

For example, a production floor had a motorized winder controlled by software written in the early 1980s. It used the processor speed for timing loop control. The time it took the processor to count from 1 to 1,356,332 was the correct delay to allow for the motor's response. When that computer died, we replaced it. With a faster computer, of course. Which promptly failed because the processor counted to 1,356,332 much faster than the motors could respond. This resulted in a search for an old computer to keep it going. The company lived with that situation for years because replacing the motors and controllers on the winder was too expensive. And rewriting the software never got high enough on the priority list.

5. *"Can't we just push the prototype into production and use it for a while?"*

Prototype projects are used to prove a design concept or to determine if a major risk mitigation will work. We put all our focus on the critical areas, leaving hacks and shortcuts everywhere else. It's just a prototype, right? It isn't the real system!

I wrote a prototype application back in the day that connected two systems together. There was a simple UI to see the data movement. There was no error checking, it was hard coded to my account, and the UI just pretended to make the data change to show the concept.

I gave it to the user, explaining that it was just a prototype, and scheduled a meeting for a few days later. When I got to the meeting, there were five additional people in the room. They had all started using the system for real and had a list of changes they wanted to see in the new system. One of them, almost apologetically, pointed out that sometimes the application was not saving their changes. Sometimes? The prototype was *never* saving their changes. Sigh.

In the end, I convinced the users I needed more time to finish the application. However, there were still a handful of items I didn't complete and, yes, they caused problems down the road.

The two reasons most often given for accepting some level of Technical Debt are, unfortunately, the two most valid: time and money. The standard joke is "We don't have time to fix it today but we will make time to fix it tomorrow." The unfortunate reality is that this will be true for any organization at some level.

The fight against Technical Debt is constant. We will make tradeoffs and accept risks daily. Some will turn out wrong and others will be right.

So how do we think about these decisions in a way that at least tries to make it better? How can we eliminate Technical Debt? To be clear, we can't, but we can be more intentional about managing it.

We can use risk management techniques. Having a good feel for likelihood and severity helps. If we get in the habit of thinking about the future with those two lenses, we might avoid the worst Technical Debt.

We can also use Focus & Finish techniques (chapter 3). Making sure that all the little details get taken care of at the end of a project before moving on to the next project. Finance makes sure that the books balance down to the penny. Human Resources makes sure that forms and paychecks are correct. IT departments need to apply the same sense of diligence to finishing changes.

Technical Debt is a reality for us. We can't prevent it. All we can do is to be aware of it and the future costs from it, and do our best to minimize it.

Technical Debt is a reality for us. We can't prevent it. All we can do is to be aware of it and the future costs from it, and do our best to minimize it.

Part 2

Business

CHAPTER 7

BUSINESS OVERVIEW

Now that we have covered a few foundational concepts, we will move into the next three parts of the book: Business, People, and Technology.

I put Business first because I believe that IT leaders must have a strong understanding of the business in order to succeed. There will always be those in our departments that know the technology at a deeper level than we do. There may be those that work really well with the people in the company.

But those that lead the IT organization need to have the deepest understanding of the organization's business in all of IT. As I will explain, this is *our most important job.*

If you have a weak understanding of the business, you will fail as an IT leader.

I will also cover the relationship between the business and the IT department, how everything boils down to the business processes, and how to identify and manage the work.

If you read only one part of the book, read this one. You can be good at People and Technology, but if you have a weak understanding of the business, you will fail as an IT leader.

CHAPTER 8

BUSINESS & IT

The point of our IT department is to help the organization succeed. To do this, we need to understand that organization and the world it operates in. In addition, we must understand technology products, services, and trends enough to know how to apply them to our organization. We must understand the overlap between business and technology. That is where the IT department lives.

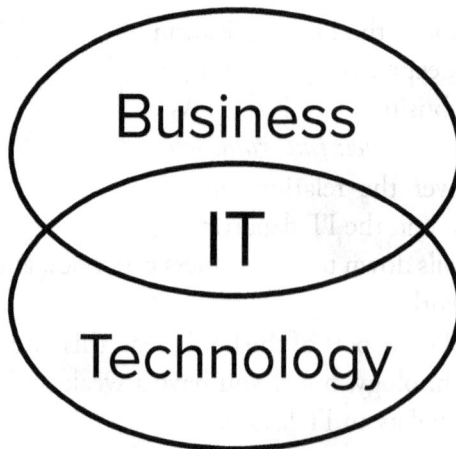

The Business/Technology Venn diagram shows the role the IT department plays in the organization. The Business circle represents the organization and the environments it operates in. The Technology circle represents the entire technology industry. It is impossible to know everything about either circle, especially Technology. Both have a current state and both are changing.

The IT department sits in the overlap of the two circles. IT is an integral part of the business, and IT lives in the technology world.

IT must understand the needs, wants, and requirements the business has. IT needs to understand the strategies in place to meet the organization's goals. IT needs to have a strong relationship with the rest of the business. In today's increasingly computerized world, the impact of technology is so profound that the leader of the IT organization needs to be part of the team determining and executing a strategy for the organization.

IT must understand the capabilities and costs of the technology available today and coming tomorrow. IT must understand trends and fads. IT must understand the role vendors play, and how to manage them.

Let's look in more detail at the two circles of the Business/Technology Venn diagram. Then we will look at the important overlap between them.

Understanding the Business

Consider the top circle. A business doesn't exist as a single snapshot. An organization of any size is a complex entity with many moving pieces. There are external and internal forces that create constant change. The better we understand these forces, the better decisions we make as the IT leader.

Here are some examples of the external forces that we need to understand:

- What are our competitors doing? Is our company winning or losing against them? Why? Can we expand market share?
- How is our industry changing? Is it relatively stable or is there tumultuous change occurring?

- How are Customer demands changing? Customer demands in any industry are always changing. Do we know what those changes are?

- How are industry or government regulations changing? Are the laws we operate under changing? What upcoming regulatory changes will force us to change how we do business?

- How is our potential employee base changing? One example is new graduates' comfort with technology. Another is the ubiquity of smartphones. What strengths and expectations will those new employees bring into the company?

- Are the business' products or services what the Customers will pay for? Are they meeting the changing Customer demands?

There are also internal forces operating within the organization that we need to be aware of. Here are some examples:

- Is the organization structure correct? Are there upcoming changes that will affect how the departments work together?

- Is our employee base changing? Is it getting older or younger? Is it getting more comfortable with our ERP or is turnover keeping the comfort level low?

- How are the financials? What financial trends are there? How does our IT spending fit into those trends? Is IT spending helping or hurting? Where does the company need to invest?

- How strong is the Continuous Improvement (CI) culture in our organization? Are there lots of CI projects that are putting stress on IT resources? Are there too few CI projects and the organization isn't moving ahead?

- What business processes need significant improvement so our organization continues to meet Customer demands?

These are some examples of external and internal forces that are driving change in our organization. The better we understand them, the better we can lead IT to be an important part of the changes.

Understanding the Technology

Now let's move to the bottom part of the Business/Technology Venn diagram.

Looking at technology, we see again that there are external and internal forces. Let's look at the external forces first.

- What fundamental shifts are happening? Over the years, we have seen mainframes, departmental computers, personal computers, mobile, and cloud. There will always be one or two major shifts going on. Keep an eye on them.

- What are vendors doing with the products and services we are using? Are they abandoning them? Enhancing them? What acquisitions are they making and how will that impact what we can, or must, buy from them?

- How is a specific product space changing? Are there new ideas or advances influencing the products? For example, anti-malware products change frequently as attacks get more sophisticated. Reporting products require less technical knowledge to use and support a wider range of data inputs.

- What new vendors are showing up on the market? How are they different? Are they new companies or existing companies moving into new market spaces?

And here are some examples of internal technology forces:

- What is our application portfolio? Do we have an existing list of all applications? Do we know where and how they are used? Do we include the Shadow IT applications?

- What applications or versions are obsolete? Which ones are going to be obsolete? How will that impact our team's ability to support them?

- Which applications are underutilized? Why? Does it matter?

- Which applications have new or additional features that would be useful to our organization?

- Are we paying maintenance for software but not getting our money's worth?
- Are we current on our operating systems?
- If we develop custom software for internal use, what is happening with the development environment? Are we using current or outdated tools? Microsoft's Visual Basic 6 became immensely popular, but then companies did not upgrade, resulting in a lot of old programs that needed old tools to fix bugs or add improvements.

I go into Technology in much greater depth later in this book. For now, consider that we frame the technology by the impact on the business.

Understanding the Overlap

Once we have a good handle on the Business and Technology, let's look at the overlap. The place where the IT department lives.

First, we should understand how well our current technology meets the business expectations and processes. Understanding this gap will point us to the technologies we need to implement or eliminate. For example, an organization that doesn't have common data definitions needs a different technical solution than an organization that has inefficient processes.

Next, we need to understand how the processes inside our IT department impact the business. If the organization is changing fast, are the IT processes keeping up? Do we have the resources appropriate to the business and is that sufficient to provide the technology and services to the business?

Finally, the IT department is an integral part of the business. If we are doing our job right, they can't swap out our department for an outside service. There is no other group that can understand the technology and understand how to apply it to the business. The overlap in the diagram represents the value IT brings to the business. We can and should find external resources that know the technology, but we won't be able to find knowledge about our business externally. We have to know it ourselves.

As I mentioned several times in the Foundations part of this book, speed and flexibility matter. This is true for IT in general, and it is true for our specific department. What changes does the business need faster, and what technologies will they require? What technologies do we need to support those changes?

Most IT employees and leaders enjoy learning about new technology and how it's applied to the company. However, we only need to understand future technology at a high level, enough to know if and how it's useful to our company.

The flip side to all the new shiny technology is that we need to understand all the current technology used in our company. And our teams need to understand it at a level of detail that allows them to support it. If we use an outside support organization, we don't need to understand the technology as much. But we always need to understand how that technology piece fits into the larger puzzle.

Our IT department needs to understand today and tomorrow's technology. And how that technology fits into today and tomorrow's organization. What possibilities are there? What capabilities will it enable? What automation will be possible? Each technology has two high-level aspects to think about.

First there are the external aspects. What business processes will it enable? What benefits will it bring the company? Does it require ongoing detailed knowledge of how it works? For example, mobile devices have had a large strategic impact on companies but most of the internals around the data and cellular networks on the phone, how the hardware works, etc. don't concern us.

Second, there are the internal aspects. How does it work? How much does it cost? What connections will we need to other systems? Again, I will go into more detail later in the book.

Deciding how to proceed with a technology is one of the key decisions we make. Do we build up the staff that has deep knowledge of the technology? Do we use external resources? The answer isn't always clear, yet that decision will have a major impact on the company.

One important tool is to hire the deep technical knowledge that a company needs. Enabled by today's remote work capabilities, it is relatively easy to find companies that will provide that deep technical knowledge at whatever level we need.

As an example, let's look at database administrator skills. If we are a company that heavily relies on our ERP system and don't have a lot of other database systems, we may not have the need for an on-staff database administrator (DBA). The ERP system is purpose-built to the database and doesn't require a lot of tuning, patching, database changes, backups, etc.

Good DBAs are expensive and, if they are on our staff, we need to keep them busy. In this kind of environment, it is likely better to have an outside DBA resource than an internal one. We can use an external DBA a few hours a month to perform the needed work. They connect in, check the performance tools, error logs, check for updates, and do preventive maintenance tasks.

The DBA resources can also monitor vendor patches and make recommendations on which ones to implement. They can implement those patches during off hours. They can make changes needed for other applications. The organizations providing these deep technical resources may also provide the ability to dive in when there is trouble. Having a DBA resource that can help troubleshoot and get the system back up and running can be very valuable.

We must take the lead in understanding which technologies will be most useful to the company and how to best roll out that technology. Using external deep knowledge can make it possible for an IT department to do more with the staff they have.

There is sometimes the inclination to just have one of the staff learn the technology and make it work. There are many IT staff that love playing with new technology and can figure out how to implement it. And this is a legitimate approach.

Given the choice of having IT staff learn the business or learning technology, I prefer they learn the business. This is especially true in the applications group.

But given the choice of having IT staff learn the business or learning technology, I prefer they learn the business. This is especially true in the applications group.

I had a Business Analyst (BA) who had been a programmer. She made the move to BA, and she was great at it. She still enjoyed writing code, but it wasn't in the company's best interest for her to spend her time there. We kept her focused on BA responsibilities and had her direct the developers. We hired external deep programming knowledge and kept her focused on the organization. We got the benefit of her development experience and the capacity of outside developers. By leading several developers, she made a bigger impact on the organization with her ideas and designs. This allowed us to move faster with this technology. And she was more satisfied with her job.

To review, it is much easier to find a deep knowledge of technology outside the company. It is much harder, effectively impossible, to find a deep knowledge of the company outside the company.

A company succeeds, in part, by having strong and flexible business processes that are constantly being improved. The BAs live at the heart of that. As a result, they end up having the broadest knowledge of a company's business processes. Individual departments will know parts of a process deeper. For example, Customer Service will know the order entry process better than the BAs, but the BAs will have a better understanding of how the data flows through the company into and out of the Customer orders.

I believe an excellent team of Business Analysts will know the business processes of the company better than any other department in the organization.

I believe an excellent team of Business Analysts will know the business processes better than any other department in the organization.

CHAPTER 9

HOW SHOULD BUSINESS THINK ABOUT IT?

The IT Department is part of the engine that drives business. It is part foundational, part enabler, and part accelerator. We can think of IT spending as a throttle controlling how fast a company leverages technology. Sometimes faster, sometimes slower.

Sometimes the company doesn't see IT as a helpful partner in the process to improve the company. *"The business will figure it out and let IT know the changes that need to happen."* This happens when the business doesn't perceive that IT adds value in that process. This is not uncommon, and I have worked at a few of these companies.

It is frustrating because the expected solutions that come into IT are rarely the best solutions. They are often problematic and are missing some important implications. The business will identify a solution that overlooks other faster and cheaper solutions. Or it solves a problem for their particular area, but will cause lots of problems downstream in the business. Or they believe there is a simple solution that IT can deliver quickly. *"This can't be that difficult."*

When that happens, we get into tough conversations and IT has to be the bad guy and ends up with a reputation as unhelpful. We get frustrated because if they had just talked to us or our team, we could have told them all this at the beginning and saved them lots of time.

However, if we look at it from the business' point of view, we can understand where they are coming from. Part of the value that IT should bring to the table is understanding of the business process in the company. How many times have we taken the opportunity to show that knowledge and use it to help solve problems? The responsibility is not with the rest of the company to believe IT understands the business. The responsibility is on us to show that we understand it. Frequently.

> *The responsibility is not with the rest of the company to believe IT understands the business. The responsibility is on us to show that we understand it.*

Sometimes we have to do this informally, with hallway conversations or side meetings. Sometimes we have to insert ourselves or an IT member into early scoping conversations on a project. We have to change how our department talks to make it less about the technology and more about the business process.

Can we sit in a meeting with a department, contributing to the discussion, and not mention technology at all? Can we re-state the business problem in our own words without talking about the technology?

This takes time and isn't easy. We must look for the opportunities to be involved in those earlier discussions and make the most of them.

Once the rest of the business has a good idea of what IT can do and views IT has a partner in running and improving the company, how should the business think about IT? The best analogy is the throttle on a car.

Throttle for Change

Most business process improvements require IT involvement. If the business wants to go faster on business process improvements, then IT can be a bottleneck. Increasing resources in IT will allow for more business process improvements.

There are two ways an organization can increase resources in IT: headcount (internal or contract) or business support. Business support refers to the resources available to work with IT to create requirements, answer questions, test solutions, and help with the rollout.

Like the throttle on a car, more throttle means more speed. More IT ability to deliver functionality means faster process change for the business.

Having more people — stepping harder on the throttle — will allow the business to go faster. To change faster. To improve faster.

This throttle concept also applies to parts of the company. If leadership decides that a particular department needs significant improvement, more IT activity can happen in that area.

We might ask: How Do We Get More Support For IT? This is actually a bad question. It isn't about how we get more support; it is about how we can better support the business. Staff groups (IT, HR, Finance, etc.) need to understand the overall vision of the business and take the correct actions.

This often conflicts with what best practices in our department tell us. For example, in HR best practices a comprehensive succession plan is important for the long-term health of the company. And it is. But it isn't always the best for a particular company. A smaller, more lightweight version of succession may satisfy the needs of a particular organization.

So what does this mean for IT? First, we should keep up on best practices. Trade magazines, peer organizations, and websites can be useful. Industry gatherings with seminars, webinars, and open bars give us the chance to talk with others. Stay connected with peers through lunches or phone calls. Keep up on new technology, what others are implementing and why, what problems people are having and how they are solving them. I have been fortunate to be a part of several vendor-free organizations made up entirely of IT professionals. These organizations are great for staying aware of how our peers are handling their IT world.

We should match a sense of where the industry is going with a sense of what is happening within our company. This means big picture things like culture, identity, market position and shorter-term internal factors like company improvement efforts. For each department, we should know what is important to them and what they are trying to change or improve.

We should have a good idea what changes are happening in the industry and the issues and responses of peers at other companies. We need to understand how our company works and what department managers are trying to do with their areas. We must understand the culture of our company and what top leadership is trying to do.

For each department, we should know what is important to them and what they are trying to change or improve.

What do we do with this understanding?

Stay connected with the organization's leaders and understand what they are trying to do. Show that we understand the challenges facing the organization and that we can contribute to finding solutions. Earn a place on the leadership team.

Merging all of this together isn't a one and done thing. Just as we need to work to stay up to speed on technology, we need to work to stay up to speed on the organization. If we can build habits to support this, we will be better off. Such habits may include updating our teams with business information, regularly attending various department meetings (listening only!), and regular conversations with the leaders of the company.

The title of this chapter is *How Should Business Think About IT?* In the end, the business needs to think of IT as a throttle for change and a group that can contribute to business challenges, and also the experts on using technology to solve those challenges.

Chapter 10

OUR MOST IMPORTANT JOB

Our most important job duty is to understand the business well enough to lead the IT department to deliver the services necessary to meet the business needs. Yes, our most important job is to look outside our department at the larger organization.

As the leader of the IT department, we lead a team with lots of connections with the rest of the business. We lead a team that supports the technology and process needs of the entire business. We will make priority decisions and resource allocation decisions that impact the rest of the business. How can we do these things if we don't understand the business?

> *Our most important job is to look outside our department at the larger organization.*

We can't.

We can only lead IT well if we have a strong understanding of the business. This understanding will help us see what may come at IT in the next month, next quarter, or next year. Knowing the changes the business is facing tells us what new technological solutions should be on our radar or what applications won't be able to keep up with those changes. Knowing the company strategy tells us what projects and other changes will be important. We can put people and technology in place to support those decisions.

As IT leaders, we should make valuable contributions to the business decision and leadership. We need to know a lot more than just IT to do that. There needs to be a fundamental understanding of business. Learn business concepts or get an MBA. Know how to read financials. Know how to read market information. Know what aspects of the world at large impact our Customers and why they want to buy our products. Understand our revenue stream and what it depends on.

Let's look at some other ways to build this deep knowledge of the business:

- Regular conversations with other leaders in the company are an important source of knowledge and awareness. What changes are they trying to implement in their departments? What changes are being forced on them from outside? How are they trying to get faster or better? How well is IT meeting their needs?

- The business makes requests that our applications team implements. Pay attention to the reasons behind these changes. The members of our applications teams will know an incredible amount about the business processes of the company. Tap into that knowledge to understand the bigger picture.

- People like explaining what they do and what challenges they face in their job. Use this. If we ask questions of enough people, and listen carefully to their answers, we can understand the organization better. Much like a pointillist painter, we can create a large picture from the individual dots. Can we see commonalities? Is one group unknowingly making another group's job harder? Is there functionality that multiple groups can use to solve a set of problems?

- Our Help Desk people hear about problems regularly. If we teach them to be curious about the business, we can tap into that. One example might be to, after solving a problem, ask the user a brief question about their job. "*I want to learn more about our company.*

Tell me about your job." This will build up company knowledge in the Help Desk and earn respect from the business.

- Is there usage data for our applications? Does that tell us about the kinds of things that are changing? For example, people are using a particular data set more in the last six months. Another example might be the number of operations incidents rising quickly. Usage information tells us about how the organization is using the solutions our teams have put in place. This might be a signal of changes in the business that we might not otherwise see.

- Some organizations have daily cadence meetings for front-line workers. IT attendance at these meetings, even if not every day, helps IT members stay current on issues. For example, some manufacturing companies have "tier" meetings. Ten to fifteen minute meetings for everyone, followed by hierarchical meetings with supervisors and managers. These meetings allow issues to escalate in minutes instead of days. These meetings can teach us about common problems and situations. They can also give us a heads up on upcoming requests.

- People need information to do their job. If it isn't available in the way they want, they will create it themselves. Find out who creates manual reports. Why are they sending it out? Who do they send it to? What do the recipients use it for? This can tell us where our reporting systems are not meeting the needs of the organization. It also helps us understand the decisions and actions driven by the report.

There are other techniques that can be on this list. Anything that gives us more information about what is happening in the company and the outside environment will help us. The more we know about our organization, the better we can do our job. We need to take all the information, stories, and complaints and turn it into the strategies and tactics for driving the IT department. We can help the business only if we have a strong understanding of the organization.

CHAPTER 11

THE CUSTOMER IS THE ONLY CUSTOMER

There is a difference between having a customer service attitude and treating the rest of the company as "customers". Too often, however, we treat them as equivalents. This chapter explains why drawing an obvious line between the two is necessary to avoid behaviors that can hurt our organizations.

Most companies have a Customer Service department, a group of people that talk to the Customer to take their orders and deal with questions and problems. Most companies believe that this is an important part of being successful.

Ever since there have been internal departments like IT, HR, and Finance, there has been a drive for those groups to call the rest of the business "customers."

"We need to take care of our (internal) customers."

"We need to treat the rest of the company like customers to have the proper service attitude."

To be clear, I believe IT departments must have a strong customer service mentality. We exist to help the company be successful. Other departments depend on us to help them with their technology needs.

I propose that the word "customer" should never denote internal business partners or departments. Let's look at why.

First, focusing on internal "customers" takes the focus off of real paying Customers. At large companies, IT departments are so removed from the Customer they don't see how their daily activities make the business successful. I have been in meetings where there was confusion on whether the subject was external Customers or internal "customers." We should focus all employees on Customers and it should always be clear who they are. There should never be ambiguity around the word "Customer."

The word "customer" should never denote internal business partners or departments.

Next, we rarely tell our Customers "No." However, we should tell others in the business "No" when appropriate. It is important that the IT default answer should be "Yes" to business requests, but it isn't blanket acceptance of every idea that comes in the door. Sometimes an idea is not in the best interest of the company and the proper answer is "No."

For example, "Let's switch all the company computers from PCs to Macs." Or vice versa. Or, "We need to buy this expensive software suite" that only takes care of a minor problem for a few people. Or a new manager joins the company and wants to implement a new performance review system after we just rolled out the current system a year ago. When the right answer for the business is "No," the IT department needs to say "No."

However, let's consider a different scenario. An actual Customer places an order to buy our company's product at our normal price. Our sales team knows that the Customer's business plan isn't very good and likely won't survive in the marketplace. Do we tell that Customer "No"? Of course not. We take the Customer's money, provide an excellent product, and do our best to help them succeed. We might change the forecast to capture our skepticism, but otherwise, we treat that Customer like all the other Customers. And we will say "Yes" to the order.

While in both cases we respond with what is best for our company, our company is not responsible for poor decisions by our Customers. We are, however, responsible for the poor decisions we make internally.

Prioritization is different between Customers and internal business partners. Transparency of the process and results are different for Customers and IT.

For example, it is important to expose the IT prioritization process to the rest of the company. The better the company knows how the IT prioritization process works, the better everyone can work together to make sure the business makes the right improvements.

But it makes little sense to inform our Customers how we prioritize their quotes and orders. We give the outward impression that every Customer is the most important and work hard behind the scenes to make sure we meet their expectations.

Then there is the output of the prioritization process — the actual priorities themselves. We should not tell a Customer that their order is less important than another Customer. The IT department, however, should be transparent about how we prioritize.

Usually, it is a bad idea to tell a Customer that we may not get to their order because there are other orders that are more important. We may need to make internal decisions that way, but we rarely tell the Customer. We would tell a Customer a delivery date, but we wouldn't tell a Customer that their order might be late because other Customer orders are more important. We might tell the Customer about the production queue and where their order sits, but it is likely that we won't talk about how Customer importance plays a role.

We must be transparent about the IT prioritization process. We must communicate the possibility that one department's request will slip if another department's request takes longer.

Internal folks need to be told that information. If the IT department is doing work for the entire company, we prioritize the tasks based on the benefit to the company. That means that a project for Research might be more important than a project for Production (or vice versa). And it might be different next month because of changing business needs. Making sure all parties involved are aware of this is important. We would likely never have that kind of conversation with Customers.

In summary, we don't want to use the same word for two very different things. We respond to requests differently. We communicate the prioritization process differently. It is best to reserve the word "Customer" for those outside the company that pay for our goods and services with actual money. And use something like "business partner," "other departments," or other such phrases to refer to those in our organizations.

For the rest of this book, I refer to actual paying Customers using a capital "C". Customers give the company money for goods and services. Lowercase "c" customers is used to refer to the internal kind, and I will only use it briefly for comparison while holding my nose.

CHAPTER 12

IT'S ALL ABOUT THE BUSINESS PROCESSES

Everything IT does needs to support the organization's business processes. Infrastructure work, for example, networks, servers, and storage, support the entire organization. Application work can apply to the entire organization, one or more departments, or even a single business process. Understanding business processes is an important foundation we will cover in this chapter.

At its simplest, a business process is a set of steps performed by one or more people that accomplishes a task necessary for the organization to succeed. While the concepts are the same, organizations think differently about business processes. Some organizations have well defined, carefully documented processes. Other organizations have processes that are more informal, relying on people's memory to know the actions to take.

We need to understand how our company defines and manages business processes.

Process Maturity Model

Spend some time to learn the concept of a "process maturity model." There are a lot of excellent resources available, so I'll give a quick overview for now. Note the terminology and definitions will differ between different maturity models:

- Ad hoc: Individuals perform the process from memory. We have very little process documentation. Performance depends on the person doing the work. Think of a small metal milling company with a few highly experienced milling operators.

- Documented: We document and follow our processes. There is some consistency across groups of people.

- Managed: We document and measure our processes. Training is in place to ensure consistency.

- Continuously Improved: We document, measure, and improve our processes. There is a formal Continuous Improvement (CI) process in the company to identify and implement improvements.

The level of process maturity needed by our organization will depend on what business we are in and the goals of the organization. Not every organization needs the highest maturity processes. And, of course, not every process in an organization will be at the same maturity level.

Types of Processes

There are two types of processes I want to call out here at the beginning. First, the normal processes of the company that perform the work that directly provide value to the Customer. Second, there are processes that handle the exceptions from those normal processes.

A simple way to understand the difference between the two is to consider manufacturing. There is the normal process that our products go through. But occasionally, something will go wrong. There will be an exception process to handle the problem. For example, if we damage the product by incorrect handling, we may need to rework it, which is not part of the normal process.

Exception processes don't happen all the time, so training and documentation are important. In addition, one part of the exception process should provide feedback to the normal process to prevent future problems. The exception process should provide information useful in reducing future exceptions.

Examples of an exception process are deviations, non-conformant material, materials review board, or in-production engineering change orders. Each industry and company will probably have their own terms for these.

Within our IT departments, we also have normal and exception processes. So understanding these concepts will help us run our IT department better and will help our IT department better support the organization.

For normal and exception processes, we need to consider four aspects:

1. Defining the Process
2. Owning the Process
3. Monitoring the Process
4. Improving the Process

Let's look more closely at each of these.

Defining the Process

We will start with what goes into the definition of a process. There are several process definition methodologies available, but these are the parts I feel are most useful:

- Roles & Responsibilities: While we may automate some process-es completely, most processes will require one or more people to do the tasks or handle the exceptions. Defining the roles and their responsibilities helps define who will do what on a day-to-day basis.

- Inputs: Every process takes something from a process in front of it. It may be an order, it may be an insurance request, it may be a permit application. Processes always start with an input. There will be acceptance criteria. The input must meet certain requirements in order for the process to operate correctly.

- Process Steps: This is work being performed. The process can be fixed where each step is the same every time throughout the process, or the process can be variable where the steps change depending on the product going through the process. Exception processes usually have variability built into them.

- Outputs: The point of every process is to add some value to the product. We create the important value for the Customer, although sometimes there are business requirements, such as tracking labor time, that result in outputs that our organization uses internally.

- Exceptions: Every process has times when things go wrong. Something needs to be fixed or reworked. For example, a Customer form is incomplete and Customer Service needs to call to get the rest of the information. We can't always predict every exception, but we should have an idea of who will handle them when they occur.

Remember Risk Management from earlier in the book? We can use that tool to analyze a process to understand what can go wrong and what risks need mitigation.

Owning the Process

No matter how we define our processes, they must have an owner. The process owner has two primary roles: (1) monitor the process to make sure it is healthy, and (2) manage the continuous improvement (CI) process.

Note that neither of these two tasks is part of executing the process. Done right, this will not take much of a person's time. But someone needs to do it.

As an example, let's look at our own Help Desk process. The process owner watches to make sure that tickets are being recorded properly, that the Help Desk is operating fast enough, and to make sure that the problems are being resolved correctly. These are different tasks than working on tickets.

If we don't have a defined owner to a process, we have little chance of the process staying healthy. If no one is monitoring the process, we may not know when it breaks or produces bad output.

There also needs to be one person who answers questions and decides what improvements to make. While this person may, and should, involve other stakeholders in the business, it rarely works if there are multiple people in charge of the process. Someone will always need to make the tough call when people disagree.

A process owner is helpful to the processes upstream and downstream. Those process owners need someone to talk to when issues come up. Process improvements that will have a large positive impact on an organization often span multiple processes. Those process owners become the team to work on those efforts.

Monitoring the Process

How do we know if a process is healthy? Is it efficient? Are problems and exceptions being handled quickly with low stress? What is changing over time? Is it producing the correct outputs? Is the process being followed in all cases?

The bigger the process, the more important the monitoring is. The more critical the process is to the success of the company, the more important monitoring is.

Process monitoring can take different forms. The most common starting point is metrics of a simple count and duration. This gives us a sense of throughput which we can validate against demand. We can add a count of errors or rework to get an understanding of the problems that show up.

Any process metric is better when tracked. I recommend having both a short-term and a long-term graph. The short-term view helps the team perform or improve to meet the goal. How did we do this week compared to last week? It is mainly for the people running the process.

The long-term graph shows changes that aren't noticeable in the short term, like seasonal or gradual trends due to personnel or business changes. For example, we might use a trailing eight weeks for the short term and trailing three years for the long term. The long term allows process owners to see historically what has been happening and to make better long-term decisions.

The number of metrics needed for a process is always challenging. Ask ten people and we will get ten opinions. Some will want a lot of numbers and graphs; others will claim that we can't measure the process at all. Others will argue against each metric individually, saying no one metric will ever contain the entire picture of the process.

Some will point out, correctly, that metrics will change the behavior — that we will get what we measure at the expense of other parts of the process.

For example, measuring *time to close* for the Help Desk will drive faster call results, but quality may suffer if we try to close tickets too quickly. Adding a quality or satisfaction metric can provide a counterbalance. With these two metrics, we have a "go faster" motivation and a "do a better job" motivation.

Should we keep adding metrics to build up all the motivations we want? Probably not. The law of diminishing returns kicks in fast. Are we getting the benefit compared to the effort of creating and managing all the metrics? Two or three select metrics can provide better focus and motivation than a large suite of graphs and numbers that mostly get ignored.

Monitoring a business process also requires that we look at facets we can't easily measure. Here are some examples.

1. How many exceptions are taking place?

The larger the process, the more exceptions occur. Whether formally or informally, people involved will have figured out how to deal with those exceptions in several ways, all of which affect the process:

- Rely on Memory. Remember the exception and keep watching for it.

- Change the process. Remember that weird exception that happened long ago and hasn't happened since? Someone built a check for it into the process, and now the process unnecessarily takes longer.
- Add "just in case" checks. Have several people check the process just in case something slips through. This is critical for things like surgery preparation or other high-risk situations, but probably not for most of our processes.

2. Assumptions about inputs change and are no longer valid.

Over time, the assumed inputs into the process change. This can be changes that take place over several years or ones that come in the span of months. It might be as simple as input parameters being exceeded, first as a onetime thing, then gradually more frequently. Sometimes it is a temporary change, sometimes it is permanent:

- "We have never had an order for that many parts."
- "The process assumes there will be fewer than four drawings and this part has seven."
- "We don't sell through distribution, but this company wants this other company to order for them."

We initially deal with situations where parameters change as exceptions. We will update parts of the process for the new situation, but parts will only be in people's heads.

3. Assumptions about outputs change and are no longer valid.

When a department creates a certain output over a long period, the receiving process may not use it the same way. For example, a department may include a document with its deliverables, not realizing that the receiving department no longer even reads it. Both sides just keep doing what they have always done, no one the wiser.

Another example is designing a custom output for a certain customer. Over time, the customer may not need it anymore because their processes have changed. How frequently do we validate that we still require the same outputs?

4. The Game of Telephone.

At every company, there is some level of "this is how I do it" training. Since each person does the process slightly differently from everyone else, the training isn't consistent. Current employees train the new people. Over time, the trainers leave and the new people do the training. If we don't have every detail of the process documented, and we rarely do, these differences will increase over time.

telephone game

5. Capacity exceeded.

Over time, more and more things are flowing through and the process gets creaky with the load. People have to go faster just to keep up. They cut corners or let lower priority items fall out of the process.

6. Staff changes.

If we only have one person performing a certain task, we run into trouble when they leave that position. Replacements will not have any overlap with prior people, so who do they learn from? Probably the person who had to step in to cover during the gap who won't have nearly the depth of knowledge.

The above situations are hard to measure and don't make good metrics. However, to keep the process healthy, we need to watch for them and address them as needed. That, combined with a few select metrics, will help us manage the process to keep it healthy.

Exception Processes

One last thing before we finish our discussion on monitoring the process. We need to understand how frequently exceptions happen.

In manufacturing, examples include Non-Conformances, Materials Review Board (MRB) items, Deviations, and Change Orders. Other industries have their own type of exceptions.

These are a special case of processes different from the normal "get work done" processes. We need them, but we don't like them.

The only reason to categorize the exceptions is to reduce them.

We monitor exception processes with two goals in mind: (1) process the exception fast and correctly, and (2) reduce the overall number of the exceptions. This second goal differs from normal processes.

Often we try to categorize these exceptions. I propose that the only reason to categorize the exceptions is to reduce them. If we aren't using that data to reduce exceptions, then we are wasting the time people spend categorizing.

The Help Desk is an interesting example of an exception process. It may be the primary process for Help Desk folks, but the problems that come in are exceptions to someone's everyday activities. Even the requests that come in, such as new or leaving employees, needed permissions, or new equipment, are exceptions to the submitter. They aren't normal activity.

Since it is an exception process, the goals include trying to prevent future exceptions. This makes sense. Obviously, preventing future problems is an important part of Help Desk activities. But those requests that come in for permissions, equipment, etc? How can we make those easier or eliminate them? One company implemented a small application that allowed managers to reset the passwords of their employees. Funny thing — the amount of password resets went down when they had to go to their manager compared to going to IT.

Monitoring a process, including its exceptions, is important for the next step: improving the process.

Improving the Process

At this point, we have a well-defined process with an owner and we are monitoring with a small number of metrics and some attention. The last thing we need to do is continually improve the process. Continuous Improvement (CI) is an important part of moving the organization forward. Each part of the organization should have an expectation of improving their processes. Fortunately, the people executing the process are often the ones with the best ideas for improvements.

Let's look at how we can improve processes.

Improving Processes: Faster

Can we remove delays from the processes? If we examine all the steps of the process, there are probably places where the task sits and waits. It may wait in a queue, it may wait for other processes to get handled first. In either case, there is some idle time as the task waits. Removing these delays will make the process faster.

Other possibilities involve automating out the "non-thinking" part. If it is a standard check on data or steps that are the same each time, consider automating them out of the process. An example might be an engineering department that works on custom equipment. Each piece of equipment is mostly the same, but each has something unique. There are tasks Engineering has to do every time: create parts in the ERP system, general BOM organization and structure, and general routing operations to build the product. After the common tasks, they apply the unique portion of the job. Automating the common tasks to give the engineers a jump start can make the process faster.

Improving Processes: More Resilient

Errors happen. Mistakes happen. Things fail. We may need to improve a process to better handle these situations. Some examples of this can be:

- The default value in a required field on a complicated screen may get missed frequently. In fact, defaults can cause problems downstream if they don't get changed when needed.

- Terms or phrases that, in normal communication context, mean one thing, but in the system mean another. For example, a company introduced a purchase order type called "Exception1" to deal with a one-off order from one Customer. Then the business changed and more Customers wanted that order type. Eventually most orders were order type "Exception1". They changed the default to "Exception1" so order entry didn't have to change it all the time. New people had to learn that it should normally be Exception1, but in some exceptions, they should change it to Normal. Technically correct, but this way lies madness. A better solution would have been to put in the extra effort to rename both types to something new and do the training to make it stick.

- A connection to a vendor's software is problematic because it keeps changing. The particular interface is fragile and breaks every time the software upgrades. The vendor has another interface that is much more robust and can handle changes without breaking. But it will cost us money to make that change. How do we decide if the added resiliency is worth it?

Improving Processes: Fewer Exceptions

As I discussed earlier, exception handling is used to process errors or differences from the normal process. These errors are making the process take longer or cause problems.

A process needing to do more than we initially designed it to do can also cause exceptions. Needing to handle a new type of financing on a Customer order might be an example. Handling a larger part or new material through an existing machine are examples. In healthcare, perhaps there are demographic fields on a form that don't have all the options, so clients leave it blank. We can handle the situation, but since it is an exception, we will probably need extra paperwork or involvement from others.

Reducing exceptions requires analyzing the exception processes to find the ones that we can eliminate. One problem I have seen is putting too much effort into categorizing exceptions. We may choose to collect lots of data, implement hierarchies of categories, and do deep root cause analysis on 100% of the exceptions. But that is likely a waste of time and effort. Let's look at a simpler approach.

We need to categorize, just not as much as most organizations do. Go for simple with only a few categories. Use a simple way to collect the data. Sometimes tally marks on a piece of paper is a good way to start.

Second, it is the front-line people that know which exceptions are the most painful. They usually have ideas on how to eliminate the exception. Eliminate those first.

We can spend a lot of time deciding what to eliminate or we can eliminate. I usually vote for the second option. Is it necessary to do deep analysis to find precisely which category and subcategory of exception we address first? I don't think so.

Compare the two tasks: (1) ongoing accuracy of WHICH exception we should eliminate or (2) ongoing reduction of exceptions? I propose it is better to reduce exceptions than spend time figuring out what exceptions to reduce.

Of course, we don't want people wasting their time on eliminating an exception that is rare and has a low impact. Cost/benefit analysis must play an appropriate role. Just don't spend a lot of time on it. The people involved in the process know some bigger exceptions to eliminate. Start there.

Here is an analogy. If we need to move an enormous pile of dirt, we shouldn't spend a lot of time figuring out where we should shovel. Just start shoveling. We may need more shovels, but we don't need more people telling us where to shovel.

Here is a terrible analogy. If we are sitting at our campsite with a cooler full of food, and a pack of ravenous rabid raccoons attack, we shouldn't spend a lot of time figuring out which is the best raccoon to hit with the marshmallow stick first. Just start swinging and don't miss. This may or may not relate to a camping trip I once took.

Improving Processes: More Capable

Business is always changing. And we often need to expand our offerings to gain market share or meet developing Customer demands. If our business processes have hard limits built into them, expanding can be harder. We may need to go outside our existing processes to meet Customer needs.

Perhaps it is the options available when Customer Service is entering an order. Or the maximum size built into an engineering tool. Changing those limits is straightforward.

The changes can be more complicated. For example, a complex supply chain where one company orders the product, another takes delivery, and a third pays. Can our order system handle that? Can it handle that if it becomes common?

Improving Processes: Less Effort

Lean Manufacturing often drives this change. Reducing the amount of effort to do the same process has obvious benefits to the company. Eliminating some steps and simplifying others can make a big difference.

This can be challenging when downstream steps depend on the output of upstream steps. Can we get the same outputs while eliminating an upstream step?

We have covered a lot here about processes. They are how the organization gets work done and there will always be the need to improve them. How does this fit into the work that IT needs to get done? In the next couple of chapters, we will look at the work IT does and how to prioritize it.

CHAPTER 13

IDENTIFYING THE WORK

IT is in the business of applying technology to help run and improve the organization. Given the pervasiveness of technology in today's world, there are very few parts of the organization that do not use technology at all. This means that there will always be work for IT to do.

The work differs from organization to organization. Even within an organization, the work changes over time. The amount of work goes up and down but always stays in the "more than we have staff for" range. There is always pressure to do more work with the people we have. How do we manage this?

In this chapter, I will present a way to identify and categorize the work so we can do just that. The next chapter will cover how to prioritize the work.

We can group the work broadly into four types. Each type will have its own process that requires its own definition of success and metrics. Each type will also have a unique process for continuous improvement (CI).

A quick note about terminology. These are the words I use and they will probably differ from what you use. There are various IT standards (ITIL, COBIT, and others) that have other definitions. The words themselves are not as important as the concepts each one represents. Use the terms that make sense for your organization.

The four types are:

1. Help Desk tickets (fixing broken stuff)
2. Service Requests (standard changes)
3. Projects (big, unique efforts)
4. Change Requests (unique changes)

So how does our team keep all this work straight? Let's look at the four types in more detail.

Help Desk Tickets

Help Desk teams need a ticketing system to make sure that nothing gets missed or forgotten. This ticketing system will track each ticket, allowing notes, communication with the user, and tracking to completion.

There are two types of tickets. The first type, and most important, are for "broken stuff" — hardware or software that isn't working as the user expects. The second type are questions and tasks and I will cover those later. For now, I'll focus on the first: broken stuff. Someone can't do their job until we fix something. Or thinks they can't do their job until a fix or workaround are in place. Closing the ticket means that the user is back up and able to do their job, perhaps using a workaround.

Defining success for the tickets process is straightforward. Speed and Quality are the primary criteria. Did IT respond and fix the problem *quickly*? Did IT respond and fix the problem *correctly*?

These tickets should get the fastest response of all the IT work. The Help Desk must triage all tickets and take care of the more important ones first. The triage (risk assessment!) process looks at impact and severity to fix the most important tickets first. An "application down" problem that affects a large group of users should get higher priority than one person having trouble printing.

It is also important to fix it correctly. When we put a fix in place, did it really fix the problem? Or did we make it go away temporarily by rebooting? Maybe we fixed it, but how many others may have that same problem in the future?

There are also those stinker tickets. The ones that are intermittent. The ones we can't replicate. The ones that make no sense. Zombie tickets. These are the kinds of tickets that take a lot of time and investigation to fix.

One thing that has been hard for me to accept is that sometimes, we just need to shrug our shoulders and move on. The reboot doesn't fix the problem, it only masks it. But sometimes, rebooting and calling it good is the right thing. Just not too often, ok?

> The reboot doesn't fix the problem, it only masks it. But sometimes, rebooting and calling it good is the right thing. Just not too often, ok?

So a good ticket process addresses speed and quality. Let's look at metrics.

Tracking the number of incoming tickets gives us the load on the Help Desk and is the right place to start. Ideally, the number of tickets per user is going down. If not, we need to look at why.

Many IT teams use "Time to Close" as a metric. How long does it take, on average, to close tickets? Since speed matters, this is a good metric. But be careful, what we measure, we improve. That is the benefit and the curse of metrics. I have seen Help Desks that only measure speed to close and it drives the wrong behavior. Closing tickets quickly, but not necessarily correctly, becomes the driving focus.

It is important to measure quality to offset this drive for speed. Measuring speed and quality together will make sure the team keeps a good balance between the two. Most ticketing system services have a satisfaction survey built in, and it is worth turning on. They usually are very simple, with satisfactory/unsatisfactory ratings and room for an optional comment. Monitor the *percent responding* number to get a representative sample and make sure the metric stays valid.

We can also track escalations if we have a multi-level Help Desk. Understanding how the number of escalations change over time will tell us how many tickets are getting resolved by the front-line Help Desk.

So we know how to judge a good ticket process, and we have covered a few concepts behind measuring the performance. Let's look at improving the process.

To get faster, there are effectively only two approaches: reduce the time spent on each ticket, or reduce the number of tickets.

We can reduce time spent on each ticket several ways.

- Training for the Help Desk staff. This one is obvious, right?
- Automating responses from the ticketing system to present questions or information back to the user quickly and consistently.
- A simple way to look up the history of the user and/or the problem. This can be anything from making sure that solutions get entered into the ticket for future reference to a sophisticated knowledgebase.
- Don't require the Help Desk staff to enter lots of data about the ticket. Other than a description of the problem and the solution, are we actively using the other fields they have to enter?

The second way to go faster is to prevent the Ticket from being created. A best ticket is the one that doesn't happen — when the user doesn't have the problem in the first place. Ticket elimination efforts are important to allow our team to support more users without growing. For example, we were getting VPN problems from most new employees. We took two minor steps: improved the configuration to simplify setup and distributed improved documentation to all new laptop employees. Most of the problems went away with these two steps.

As I mentioned, "broken things" are one type of Help Desk tickets. Questions and Tasks are others. Questions are quickly answered or they become a task to investigate, so we really only have Tasks to consider. And most of those tasks are asking for a change. Sometimes they are standard changes and sometimes they are unique changes. Let's look at both.

Service Requests

Service Requests are standard changes. These requests come in frequently and vary only in the specifics. Examples include adding new employees, enabling VPN, providing a replacement computer, updating automated report distribution lists, and so forth.

Service Requests should have a form that users fill out to ensure standard inputs. A standard process for each Service Request is used to ensure the process has the same results each time, regardless of which person is doing the work.

Defining success for service requests focuses on the areas of speed and quality. Being able to respond to these changes quickly is a significant benefit to the organization. If we can get notification of a new employee and have everything ready for them, including hardware, software, account setup, etc., the next day, the business can move faster. The same point applies to installing an application, granting access to data, or getting a new mobile phone. The less time the organization spends waiting for IT, the better.

Being able to execute Service Requests quickly also helps our staff. These processes are often the least interesting. If we create a process to finish Service Requests quickly and efficiently, our employees can move on to other tasks sooner.

It may be tempting to create lots of Service Requests. There is a balance between the benefits of having a particular Service Request and the work needed to maintain it. Maintenance includes ensuring forms and written procedures are always correct and up to date. I strongly suggest implementing them slowly. Make sure each Service Request is built into the culture properly before rolling out additional ones.

The ticket elimination process I mentioned earlier often leads to creating or updating a Service Request. In the VPN example I mentioned earlier, we updated the New Employee Service Request to prevent future VPN tickets.

For example, if there are always a few tickets that come in when employees first use VPN, creating a Service Request to make sure VPN is set up properly and communicated, will help eliminate those tickets.

Metrics for Service Requests following the definition of success. How long does it take the team to execute them on average? How many of them get follow-on tickets because there was a disconnect with their expectations?

To improve the Service Request process, focus on streamlining it with online solutions and automation. Most help desk software systems can use forms or other ways to collect the same set of information for a particular service request. Since the steps of the process are the same each time, with only the data changing, scripting and other automation will reduce mistakes and errors.

Projects

In the world of IT work, Projects are larger efforts where IT is handling the project management task. IT Projects are typically efforts like ERP upgrades, major IT infrastructure improvements, and new system installations where the company feels that IT leading the project is appropriate.

Typically, business process projects led by the business will lead to Change Requests (covered in the next section) that IT can track and manage as discrete work elements. There is a gray area between Projects and collections of Change Requests, so we need to use our judgment on what works best.

When IT is leading the project and doing most of the work, it is better to manage it as a set of tasks rather than Change Requests.

A successful project is one that comes in on time, on budget, and meets requirements. Easy to say, harder to do. The project management methodology used will vary from organization to organization. If there is a Project Management Office (PMO) we can follow their project management methodology. If not, then we are free to use whatever methodology we wish.

project management methodologies

Metrics for projects are a challenge. Rarely do two projects have the same task list. For example, upgrading all our database servers is something that we may do once every few years. But each time we do it, the tasks list will be slightly different as the environment and personnel have changed in those intervening years.

Depending on department size, we may only do a few projects a year. Again, if a PMO exists, there will be metrics. If not, I recommend not worrying about project metrics other than schedule, cost, and deliverables.

Just because we don't have metrics doesn't mean that we can't have CI. Project CI is more straightforward than tickets, Service Requests, and Change Requests. CI for projects requires one thing: effective use of collected Lessons Learned.

Lessons Learned is a list of recommendations to future projects on how to do things better. During any project, there will be missteps or mistakes or wrong assumptions. There will also be things we did right. Keep track of both the good and the bad during the project. Also, keep a log of major project decisions and revisit them at the end to see if they all turned out to be the best choice. At the end, have a session with everyone involved in the project and collect the lessons learned. Phrase them to make them useful for future projects. For example, "Verify updated permissions earlier in the process" is better than "We had problems with getting correct permissions." Adding these lessons to the general knowledge of those in IT running projects will help make the next project better.

Change Requests

So far, we have covered tickets (broken stuff), Service Requests (standard changes like new employee setup), and Projects (large efforts with lots of tasks). The last type of IT work to talk about is Change Requests. In my experience, Change Requests make up most of the organization CI work IT does.

Think of Change Requests as all the changes the business needs IT to implement to improve a business process.

Ideally, most of the Change Requests are coming from work in the organization to improve itself. For example, Customer Service improving its order entry process may have one or two parts of the system that need changing. These come to IT as Change Requests. Think of Change Requests as all the changes the business needs IT to implement to improve a business process.

The more Continuous Improvement tasks a company does, the more Change Requests will come into IT. It may be as large as a new application and may be as small as adding a column to a report. It may have well defined and clear requirements or it may need a brainstorming session to come up with ideas.

While the line is sometimes fuzzy, Change Requests are smaller than projects and rarely have much project management overhead. There will probably be a set of tasks for a Change Request, but the list will be shorter and simpler than a project.

We can also use Change Requests to track internally generated changes. For example, replacing network switches or updating firmware on a SAN.

Like Service Requests, the definition of success for Change Requests centers on speed and quality. The faster our IT department can turn around Change Requests, the sooner our organization can improve those business processes. The faster an organization improves its processes, the better chance it has in succeeding.

The quality of a Change Request also matters. Getting the change right the first time has clear advantages. Reworking a change takes more effort and takes away from other work. Users and our team get frustrated if rework happens too often.

The challenge comes in creating metrics for Change Requests. Service Requests are, by definition, common and/or similar to each other, so there is consistency in effort and results. Change Requests do not have any kind of consistency. Work effort for Change Requests will vary from a few hours to weeks or sometimes months. Requirements can range from a couple of sentences to a large document. Deliverables can vary from a simple SQL output to a suite of tools and applications.

Measuring the quality of a new application may be measurable by the number of tickets in the first two weeks or by a satisfaction survey, but those numbers will look very different from adding a new report.

So what do we do? We want to have metrics for our Change Requests, but the work varies wildly and setting goals is difficult.

Let's look at speed first. We know when a Change Request starts and finishes. We can easily get a duration and create a rolling average. Is that number good enough? Most likely not. Whatever it is, both IT and the rest of the business will feel that it is too slow. So what do we set as the goal? How long should Change Requests take?

We could use the technique of collecting the data for a while and then setting the goal. If the rolling two-month average duration is, say, 13.8 days, then setting a goal of 10 days might be a decent first step. Keep in mind, however, that the mix of change requests will strongly influence the metric. If we get many requests to change reports, our average will improve even if our performance did not. A few larger Change Requests will make the metrics worse even if we did an outstanding job getting the work done.

Bottom line is that we have to track duration, but there are lots of caveats in understanding the numbers. Best to start somewhere and then work to improve the baseline.

Setting metrics for quality will have the same problem. Measuring quality using help desk tickets is one way, but a new report for a department will have a smaller impact than a new application for the entire organization. How do we measure quality for each of those? A "good/bad" satisfaction survey is probably the best bet, but will have a lot more gray area in the middle than tickets. Anything more complicated to measure quality will just add work to the process. Is the improvement in the quality metric worth the extra work?

The bottom line for Change Request metrics is that we can probably get duration and quality, but understanding the numbers and setting goals will be much harder than for tickets.

Let's look at how we approach CI for Change Requests. The goal is to increase the number of change requests completed. More change requests completed means more business processes improved.

How can we get more Change Requests completed?

- Look at how often the Change Requests are being completed correctly the first time. Less rework means more completed Change Requests.
- Shorten up time waiting for the business. Do more face-to-face reviews of requirements or testing.
- Break larger efforts down into smaller Change Requests. This allows the larger benefits to get into production earlier with other functionality added later. This will also help prioritization as I will cover in the next chapter.
- Add tools and utilities to speed up test data generation, data validation, and data updates.

There are a few things that we can focus on that will bring the largest improvements. Obviously, each organization will be unique, but I hope the following explains it well enough.

First, make sure that the tracking system in place for Change Requests is a light-weight process. It should be easy to add, prioritize, update, and close Change Requests. Generating metrics should not require a lot of extra work by the team.

Second, there should be a step early in the process to verify that everyone agrees on two items for each Change Request: requirements and test plan. Agreement on these two items by IT and the requesters will not eliminate scope creep or misunderstandings, but will reduce them significantly. At the very least, it makes it easier to talk about scope creep.

Remember that the requesters may not be the only ones affected by the Change Request. Involving all the stakeholders in the initial discussions is always time well spent.

Finally, focus and finish. As I discussed in chapter 3, keeping the number of active Change Requests low will improve throughput. This will be hard to do as the number of active Change Requests will trend upward because of the service mentality common in IT. We need to remind our teams, perhaps even ourselves, to stay focused on a few active Change Requests and finish them before starting the next one.

The four types of work — Help Desk tickets, Service Requests, Projects, and Change Requests — are a good way to group and manage the work that our IT department does. The process for each type will be different and have its own metrics and CI.

Now we just have to figure out how to prioritize.

CHAPTER 14

PRIORITIZING THE WORK

Read anything about task management, time management, or productivity, and they will address prioritization. Having a long list of things to do and no sense of prioritization is a recipe for wasted time.

And no one wants to waste time.

In the last chapter, I organized the IT work into four areas: Tickets, Service Requests, Projects, and Change Requests. If we are setting this up for the first time, the sheer amount of identified work tasks will overwhelm us. How are we ever going to get it all done?

> *Having a long list of things to do and no sense of prioritization is a recipe for wasted time.*

"How do you eat an elephant? One bite at a time."

That's a nice handy quote reminding us to get started and keep going. The project management world uses this quote frequently, and it is a powerful tool for understanding how to break down a big project into smaller pieces.

Nevertheless, it may not be the best analogy to use here. I would like to suggest another one. One that uses alligators.

Imagine a swamp. This swamp has alligators living in it. Lots of alligators. These aren't the cute cartoon alligators. These are your normal "don't mess with me" alligators. There are newly born alligators, there are teenage alligators, there are enormous monsters older than the hills. There are aggressive alligators wandering around, actively hunting. There are alligators that sit invisibly just beneath the surface, not bothering anyone, unless we get too close.

Sounds fun, right? Let's make it more interesting. Our job is to deal with the alligators so our organization can navigate the swamp safely.

All the work we listed in the prior chapter are alligators we need to deal with in this chapter. Don't worry, I won't overuse the analogy. Like all analogies, this one breaks down if you look too closely. Also, as I was working on this part of the book, I started dreaming about alligators and no one wants that.

So how do we prioritize all the work?

There will never be agreement across the company on what we should work on next. Some people want their stuff first. Some people want what's best for the company, but their particular view of what's best differs from others.

Everyone wants to be involved in the priority discussion. But only for their stuff. Most won't want to wade through all the other requests we have to prioritize. The nice ones will understand the hard challenge of managing these priorities. The less nice ones won't care and will just want their stuff done.

The only thing we can count on is that there will always be some that are unhappy with the prioritization. But all is not hopeless. There are some approaches that, while not universally praised, are better to implement and explain to the company.

We will start first with tickets. Prioritization of Help Desk tickets is straightforward. When multiple things break, fix the ones that can get more people back up and running first. For example, we should urgently fix anything that stops us from delivering to our Customers. While prioritization of tickets can get hard when the ticket count gets high, the prioritization issues are straightforward.

Likewise, Service Requests are fast and often have external deadlines (for example, new employee setup) so prioritization is less important. We prioritize Service Requests with deadlines and a first-in-first-out queue.

Prioritizing projects can be more complicated, but given the uniqueness of each project, there will be unique prioritization conversations each time. I would note that the line between Projects and Change Requests is very vague. I draw the line to have very few large projects and more Change Requests. You might do it differently, however, the prioritization concepts below still apply.

That leaves us with Change Requests. This is one of the most difficult prioritization problems in IT. There are a wide variety of Change Requests and a wide variety of opinions on how to prioritize them.

Aspects of Prioritization

The rest of this chapter will be about prioritizing Change Requests. I will present three important considerations followed by a discussion of some prioritization processes. I will end with a special note about prioritizing IT Improvement work.

There are three things we need to consider when prioritizing: Prioritization Scope, Types of Estimates, and Opportunity Cost.

1. Prioritization Scope

People have a wide variety of opinions on prioritization. No surprise there. These opinions have three major components to them.

First, how big is their vision? Do they think in terms of impact on themselves? Or do they think in terms of impact on the entire organization?

And second, what time frame are they looking at? Are they thinking about next month or are they thinking about three years from now? Hopefully, the higher up the leadership, the further out the vision.

Finally, how do they view what is important to them, to their department, and to the company? Companies are complex things, and people will have different opinions about the importance of various changes.

Individuals know their own area really well, especially the current problems. This will drive their prioritization decisions to focus more on their specific group and the shorter time frame.

One example of this smaller viewpoint is the "fix or eliminate" problem. Let's look at an example of a product return that comes through Customer Service. Customer Service fills out a form when the parts come in. This form is used to collect information from the Customer. We use this information elsewhere in the company to process the return. A Change Request comes in to automate this form. The people involved in this problem every day see this as valuable as it will save them a lot of time and improve the quality of the information. The fix is to convert a manual process to an online process. Sounds like a good idea, right?

Well, maybe not. What if, over the last few years, other internal processes had changed, and that information wasn't really being used anymore? What if, over time, we had made the paper form much more complicated that it needed to be? If we look at this Change Request from a larger organizational view and a longer time frame view, maybe we don't need the form anymore. Or maybe it can be simplified substantially. Maybe it is better to change the process to eliminate the form rather than try to automate it.

This "fix or eliminate" situation comes up frequently when looking at exception processes. Over time, the exception processes will have a tendency to get more complicated to deal with more exceptions. Change Requests will be submitted to support this expansion. However, wouldn't it be better to put that same effort into reducing the number of exceptions? It is a judgment call, but sometimes it is better to eliminate part of a process or the need for the Change Request than to implement it.

There are other factors that play into the larger Change Request prioritization scope. Does the company have important improvement goals? If so, that should influence which Change Requests get done. Does a Change Request increase the organization's speed or flexibility?

Government regulation is also a consideration. For example, the CMMC model for the defense industry. The FDA medical device regulations have rules around software that impact prioritization. PCI (credit cards) and HIPPA (health information privacy) also can play a role.

As IT leaders, we need to have the long view. The better we understand the entire business, the easier it will be for us to look at the list of Change Requests and know which will have the larger impact on the business.

We also need to understand the long-term effects of prioritization decisions. There are complications that only will show up in the long term. Here are some examples:

- Does a CR bring in a new technology that will have a long-term impact on the company? Often we justify new technology on the first project so everyone focuses there. Our job is to keep the other possibilities alive in the business' mind.
- Does the CR leverage old technology that is going away? When do we cut off that old technology and force all new CRs to use the new technology? What if the new technology isn't quite available yet? Or maybe it takes longer to implement the CR?
- Does the CR help or hurt the overall security model?
- Does the proposed solution add complexity to the maintenance effort? The desire for flexibility often brings more complex solutions that require extra effort to debug and maintain.

The prioritization scope is something to be aware of all the time as we watch the prioritization process work. We will find ourselves with opinions on certain Change Requests. There aren't many people in any organization that have a long-term view of the entire organization, so we will need to speak up often on this.

2. Type of Estimating

Getting estimates is a necessary part of IT life. How long will it take? How much is it going to cost? How much money will we save? How big is this effort? These questions are part of the cost/benefit discussion. To decide if a change is worth doing, we need to have some sense of how much work it will take to implement.

There are different times in the process where these questions get asked. Someone gets an idea and wonders if it is good. That comes very early and doesn't need much precision on the answer, which is good because there are no requirements, just an idea. Later on, a change request may be on the list and we need a better estimate because it is getting closer to the top of the priority list. And then there are the extensive projects, the major system upgrades, the major development efforts that end up being capital projects and require detailed plans.

I divide estimates into three types. The name refers to how long we should spend creating the estimate:

- The Five Second Estimate
- The Thirty Minute Estimate
- The Four Hour Estimate

Let's look at each of these, how they work, and when they are appropriate. I have used most of these in my career, some of them more or less depending on my team and the situation.

The Five Second Estimate

I usually use this in the idea stage. Someone has an idea for a change and wants to know if it is even a good idea. No details are available, we need no precision. These ideas can pop up anywhere. And, to be honest, these could be random ideas from the manager (yes, us!) and may not even be good ones. The more ideas we have, the better able we are to solve problems creatively. But we also need to test the ideas quickly.

So imagine we have this awesome idea. What we really need in that moment is the Five Second Estimate. The level of detail for this type of estimate is "order of magnitude." I usually ask, "Will this take hours, days, weeks, or months?" I don't care how *many* hours, days, weeks, or months, I'm just looking for a quick order of magnitude to evaluate the idea. I do not want them investigating this idea at all and just want a quick answer.

Making these kinds of estimates will make the team uncomfortable. Keeping it focused on the order of magnitude helps, but, by definition, we know very little about the idea, so we make lots of assumptions. The more we ask them for these estimates, and give the team a chance to explain their thinking, the more comfortable they will get. Experience is the best way to get better at these quick estimates.

Communicating these estimates to the business can be tricky. In this case, framing it in the context of magnitude is important. It will tempt us to put a number in front of it. Don't. In fact, be very careful about spreading the five second estimate outside of IT. Our team spent five seconds making the estimate and probably made some big assumptions we are not aware of.

Over time, we will develop a sense for how our team thinks about ideas and a better sense for how they estimate.

The Thirty Minute Estimate

The Thirty Minute estimate is for when we need more detail. A little more time, a little more accuracy. Listing the major tasks, documenting the assumptions, and investigating a few options will take more time and give a better answer. This length of time allows us to identify and mitigate a few of the major risks.

Change Requests that will take weeks should get this level of estimate before starting. It allows us to provide a better expected completion date, and then we can use risk management to stay out of trouble.

This is the one that typically gets used if our organization uses a cost/benefit approach to Change Requests.

The Four Hour Estimate

This level of estimate is for the larger projects. This is a standard project plan with resources and a mostly complete task list. Everyone significantly involved should have input on this. Learn a project management tool or how to use a spreadsheet to track tasks, resources, dependencies, etc. We typically do a full risk assessment and mitigation plan for this level of estimate.

3. Opportunity Cost

Opportunity cost is what we are giving up by taking a particular path. We put something on the list to do and it gets to the top. The people assigned start to work on it. In doing so, they are not working on anything else. Opportunity cost is understanding the cost of what they are not working on.

Opportunity cost should be a tool in our prioritization arsenal. If we assign person A to change request B, the opportunity cost is the work that A could have completed if we had instead assigned them to change request C.

opportunity cost

Let's look at a specific situation to illustrate the point. One of our staff, let's call him Lonnie, is about to start a change that will improve a set of reports for the Customer Service department. That morning, a bug pops up in the system, and Lonnie is the best one to fix it. Identifying and deploying the fix takes three days. During those three days, Lonnie is not working on those reports. The intentional decision to delay the reports for three days is the opportunity cost.

> *Opportunity cost is understanding the cost of what they are not working on.*

Is it worth delaying the reports? Depends on the reports and the bug, right? If the bug affects five people and there is a workaround and the reports are for a new process change that is rolling out next Monday, that opportunity cost may be too high and it is best to keep Lonnie on the reports. But if the bug affects the financials and the reports are minor tweaks to existing reports, we might pay the opportunity costs without hesitating.

So keep that concept in mind: what are we choosing not to do?

Here are some situations to think about.

Opportunity cost is why our team will want to move on to a new effort rather than completely finishing what they are working on. The tasks left to the end of the project may not bring as much immediate value to the organization as the next project. Those tasks that "we will do

after going live" must be completed to finish properly, but the new shiny Change Request feels like it is more important.

There are often multiple solutions to a change request. Multiple ways to implement the change. Multiple technical solutions. Each will take a different amount of time and have different long-term benefits. We won't be able to make those choices solely on the merits of the various choices. We will need to consider what else the team has to work on. If there is something critical coming next, we may have to pick the shorter duration effort to move to the next one quickly. Other times, the project is very important, and the long-term cost of ownership is significant enough that we swallow the opportunity cost.

Another example. Consider a situation where a team member, Elijah, can complete a Change Request two ways, both meeting the requirements. The fast way (say, two weeks) gets the job done, but the longer way (say six weeks) implements the groundwork for the expected future. The fast way may cause future problems, as Elijah will need to do additional work when the future change happens. The business knows they want to do the future change, but doesn't know when. They say "sometime in the next year".

If Elijah takes the fast way, he can get other Change Requests completed in that four-week difference. The benefit of the longer way is less work in the future. But the opportunity costs are those Change Requests Elijah might get done in those four weeks. Elijah needs to compare the benefit of the longer, and better, solution to the cost of delaying the other Change Requests.

It is never a nice, easy mathematical calculation. It will always be a judgment call. And, as we all know, not everyone will be happy with the decision. That comes with the job.

Another factor to consider when looking at opportunity costs is the skills of the people involved. Not everyone can do every Change Request. Because of skills, technology, or history, there can be Change Requests that only a certain person can complete. What else could they be working on? We may always send a certain type of request to one person because they are great at it and get it done quickly. And then the number of those requests grows and comes to dominate their time. What else could they be working on? Do they enjoy working on those tasks? Is employee burnout a possibility?

Reducing opportunity costs is a good reason for cross-training people into different areas. Increased cross-training provides us with more options when making assignments.

Prioritization Processes

Prioritization is an ongoing process. We can't make a list once and call it good. Our teams will complete Change Requests and go on to the next ones on the list. New Change Requests will come in continually. Prioritization needs to happen regularly and therefore needs a process around it.

Before we talk about the process, let's talk about who does the prioritization. Over my career, I have tried both doing all the prioritization myself and having the team do it. There are pros and cons of each. If I do it, there is a single holistic view, but the team will continually come to me for updates. I found that if the team prioritizes; they prioritize faster with the minor downside that they might not make the same decisions I would.

It takes time and effort to teach the team the framework and decision points for making the priority decisions, but once the team understands this, the process works better. Teach them about the larger business priorities, make sure they know the important improvement goals, and let them prioritize all the requests that come in. This puts the brainpower of our team to work.

I have found that teams that do the prioritization are much more engaged in the business. They can handle the prioritization conversations with others in the business by themselves. And they handle exceptions, and the potential fires better. I stay involved at a top level to make sure they have my input as I work with the business.

By teaching our team and letting them do the prioritization, we have to let go. They will not always prioritize the same way we would. Sometimes we have to take a deep breath and focus on how well they are doing overall and not on a specific prioritization issue. Yes, sometimes we play the "manager card" and dictate what to do, but I found that using it as a teaching moment by explaining my rationale shows them something they had missed. They often have a good reason for disagreeing, and we both learn something. This is a win/win.

Let's look at the major types of prioritization processes:

- Ad hoc Prioritization
- Department Prioritization
- Company Prioritization

Ad Hoc Prioritization

As the saying goes, the squeaky wheel gets the grease. IT departments that are using ad hoc prioritization are deciding on the fly which Change Requests to implement. Those that complain the loudest get their request moved to the top of the queue.

There might be a sense of what is important to the company, but we haven't documented it. And we don't really use it to prioritize. We make prioritization decisions by the seat of our pants.

There may not even be a list of all the outstanding requests we can prioritize. Maybe there is something written on a whiteboard or in an email sent last week.

Even worse, they may stop the current top priority to start the next "do it now" task. Partially completed Change Requests end up strewn all over the department, providing the rest of the organization with more reasons to be unhappy with IT.

Obviously, this is a not a pleasant situation. No one is happy except for the squeaky wheel.

So if this is how our company prioritizes, how do we improve?

Department Prioritization

The next most common prioritization is at the department level. Departments come in lots of sizes and shapes, and each organization is unique.

Employees are usually aware of the issues in their department more than they are aware of the issues in the organization. This is not a surprise. We understand our own needs and often can extrapolate out to our coworkers. We understand how our department fits into the larger picture, even if we don't understand the larger picture. For example, if an employee knows a process change will improve their department, they can usually explain how that benefits the organization overall.

We start department prioritization with regular meetings with the department leaders to prioritize change requests. The two important tasks for these meetings are identifying the most important changes on the list and removing changes from the list. We won't need to prioritize the entire list, only the work that the IT department will get to before the next meeting.

This method results in multiple department priority lists. That leaves IT in the position to decide. This is better than ad hoc because we have information on each department's top priority. Regularly completing the top priority Change Request for each department gets closer to the elusive goal of prioritizing what is more important for the entire company.

Deciding between departments isn't easy. A few department leaders will look at the larger picture. Most will have a hard time looking at all the changes together and deciding which is most important for the organization. A common response is, "I don't understand that group well enough to have an opinion on how to prioritize their stuff."

Knowing the organization well puts IT in an excellent position to know which department changes will have a larger impact on the organization.

Company Prioritization

Some organizations try to move to a company-wide prioritization process for IT projects. The idea is to get the largest, most important work identified and prioritized at a company level.

If you are familiar with the "rocks in a jar prioritization" concept, this is an attempt to set the rocks at a

rocks in a jar story

corporate level. We set up a team of organizational leaders, meet regularly, and make sure that everyone agrees on the largest IT priorities. Often called the "IT Steering Committee," this team will ensure the largest IT priorities match that of the organization.

At some level, it would be ideal if there was no IT prioritization list, if the IT prioritization was simply the organization's priority list. The organization's priority list would drive changes that the IT department implements.

The steering committee provides a forum for IT to present larger issues, implications of decisions, and financial effects of various projects and options. It allows the organization's leaders to discuss the pros and cons of each project. Agreement on priorities by the organization's leaders can remove implementation difficulties.

> *It would be ideal if there was no IT prioritization list, if the IT prioritization was simply the organization's priority list.*

The strength of this method is that the steering committee prioritizes the largest projects. The weakness of this method is they prioritize nothing else.

In some organizations, a steering committee meets once per quarter or so and prioritizes the "rocks." The more time IT spends completing the large, impactful projects, the better we meet the organization's needs. However, our departments are not just working on the rocks.

There is always a long list of other Change Requests the organization needs. These Change Requests can be, for example, report changes, process changes, or data updates. We don't want the organization's top leadership prioritizing this lower priority work. They have more important ways to spend their time.

So if we go the steering committee route, keep in mind that we will still need to have a prioritization method for dealing with everything other than the rocks.

A Special Note About IT Process Improvements

Before we leave the topic of prioritization, I want to acknowledge the special challenge of prioritizing IT improvements. Some examples might be to improve new employee onboarding or improving the prod/test/dev sync process.

Like the rest of the organization, we expect IT will improve its internal processes. To do so requires the same IT resources that are making improvements for the rest of the company. The opportunity cost for improving an internal IT process is that it delays some non-IT improvement. Everyone is unhappy about that. IT wants to help more and everyone else wants their Change Requests completed.

IT is so busy making everyone else's processes better that we don't take time to improve our own processes.

An old proverb says that shoemaker's children don't have shoes because the shoemaker is busy making them for everyone else. This also applies to us. IT is so busy making everyone else's processes better that we don't take time to improve our own processes.

It won't always be popular, but we must make sure we take the time to improve our internal processes. There will be some opportunity costs in the short run, but the improvements should benefit the organization over the longer run.

Wrap Up

No matter how we do it, prioritization is a no-win situation. It is not possible to make the entire organization happy with the prioritization choices we make. The best we can do is to be transparent with the process we are using and decisions we make. Listen to the objections and continually try to improve the prioritization process.

The best result is to have the leadership of the organization agree that IT is working on the most important tasks.

Part 3

People

CHAPTER 15

PEOPLE OVERVIEW

While most IT books and articles focus on the technology, we know that having the right people working well together is more important than having the right technology in place. With talented people and mediocre technology, we can still make a big impact on the company's success. With mediocre people and great technology, well, we probably won't have that great technology very long and we and our team will become order takers instead of strong business partners.

> With talented people and mediocre technology, we can still make a big impact on the company's success.

In this part of the book, I will talk about the people part of running IT. The first chapter is *Managing Ourselves* because, in the unintentionally wise words of the airline warnings, we need to put on our own oxygen mask before helping others. Put another way, we need to make sure we are in a good place before we can be an excellent leader for the team.

The next chapter covers the aspects of *Leading the IT Team*. The Management section at the local bookstore probably has several books on managing people. While they are useful, the specific combination of the demands of an IT department and the kinds of people that are interested in working in an IT department has some additional complexities.

The last chapter will cover *Building the Right Team*, including interviewing, leadership styles, interns, and external resources.

CHAPTER 16

MANAGING OURSELVES

Managing ourselves can be harder than managing others. In related news, doctors and nurses make terrible patients. I'm married to a nurse, so I know this to be true. It is easy to wave it off, convinced that we are in good shape and don't need any help.

Trust me, improving as a leader is a lifelong journey. As a leader, we are never as good as we think we are. But take heart, because we probably aren't as bad as we think we are.

This chapter contains topics I feel are important for an IT leader but are missing from general leadership books.

One quick note before I get into it. These are not topics that I am an expert on. Since I first understood them, I have been working to close the gap between what I know and how I behave each day. As Walt Whitman wrote in *Song of Myself, 51*:

> *Do I contradict myself?*
> *Very well then I contradict myself,*
> *(I am large, I contain multitudes.)*

Walt wasn't in IT, but he knows a thing or two about the difference between our ideals and our reality. Since we never reach perfection, let's look at the never-ending journey. Here is a list of principles I have learned over the years:

- Focus & Finish for IT Leaders
- Monkeys Everywhere!
- Constant Decision Making
- Walkabouts

Remember, this is not an exhaustive list of how to be an excellent leader. Think of this as some things *necessary* to be an excellent IT leader.

Focus & Finish for IT Leaders

Running the IT department requires managing lots of different tasks. These tasks range from long term technological decisions to helping a visiting Customer figure out how to connect their computer to the guest wireless. Managing budgets, IT processes, and keeping tabs on all the activity in the department can lead to hundreds of open tasks on our To-Do list. Throw in the mass quantities of email we receive and staying on top of everything can be overwhelming.

Focus & Finish applies to us specifically as much as it applies to our teams. So what does it mean for us on a day-to-day basis?

On a day-to-day basis, one truth is that we won't have time for everything, no matter how many hours we put in. There are only two things to do in that case: (1) use our time wisely, and (2) work on the most important tasks.

Using our time wisely is one of those things easy to say and hard to do. But it is simple to start: control interruptions to allow longer periods of time to work.

Start small. Notifications from the computer and phone are not helpful. Turn most of them off. We don't need to know when each email comes in. Instead, set a few times a day to work through email. Smartphone notifications are even worse.

We control our devices, don't let it be the other way around.

Every time I install a new app, I turn off all notifications. We control our devices, don't let it be the other way around.

IT leaders get lots of calls from vendors. Don't answer them. Make sure caller ID works right and be ruthless in sending calls to voicemail.

Next up: calendars. We have all kinds of meetings, from long-term leadership meetings to project meetings to department meetings. We need to make sure we are spending our time on the things at the top of our list. Sure, there are meetings that we can't control, demands on our time that we can't do anything about.

However, there are things on our calendar that we can control. Can staff cover some meetings that need IT representation? Are the meetings efficient with agendas and goals? Do the meetings run too long? Can they be shorter and still serve their purpose? Read a little of the research on meetings. The gap between what we know to be best practice and what we are doing is usually larger than we think.

I highly recommend blocking off time on your calendar. My personal favorites to block off are Monday mornings and Friday afternoons. Monday morning lets me get organized at the start of the week. And, for reasons I don't understand, I get weirdly productive on Friday afternoons.

Last, not all hours of the workday are created equally. Portions of the day will be better for long undisturbed thinking. Other parts, not so much. I always struggle with the post-lunch slump if I am at my desk, so I try to schedule administrative tasks during that time. Since I get energy from meeting with others, I'll also schedule one-on-one meetings or walkabouts during this time.

Conversely, I use the morning for longer uninterrupted time to work on larger tasks.

If we understand when we are strongest during the day, we can structure days accordingly. We will never have complete control over our schedule, but we have more control than we think.

So now we have blocked all but the most important interruptions and taken more control of our calendar. We have more time for our tasks. Let's make sure we are working on the right things.

Focus & Finish (chapter 3) says we shouldn't have very many tasks and projects active at once. In that chapter, we talked about keeping the active tasks to a small number. As the IT leader, we will have the largest number of active tasks. That is the curse of leading the IT team.

So how do we apply Focus & Finish to all these tasks?

Delegate what we can. Own what we can't. As the IT leader, we are the only one that can manage our team. We are also the one in the position to be the primary leadership interface between the company and its technology department. Almost everything else can be a candidate for delegation.

That means we need a team we can delegate to. I'll cover that topic in the next section. We don't have to do everything that the organization *asks* of us. We need to do the things the organization *needs* of us. Taking on a few tasks besides our leadership role is necessary. But don't take on dozens of tasks. Frequent communication with our supervisor can ensure she knows our approach and has our back with others in the organization.

> *We don't have to do everything that the organization asks of us. We need to do the things the organization needs of us.*

Task management is also important. I've been to a half-dozen time management courses in my life and this is one area in which I am much better, but still challenged. I have tried lots of different ways to manage all the tasks on my plate, constantly changing as one method after another failed. All flavors of paper lists, post-its, Outlook tasks (three different times!) and various apps. My only conclusion is that task management is deeply personal and hard to maintain. Spend time to get into a groove and then do the hard work to maintain it.

I take solace in knowing that very few people use the same task-management technique for decades. Ask around. Most are always looking for a better way.

What can we let fall off our plate? We are in charge of how we best use our time to help the business and earn our salary. Tasks, requests, questions, and analysis have different priorities and rarely do we need to complete all of them RIGHT NOW.

As I mentioned before: Sometimes we need to let some fires burn so we can put out the more damaging fires. Trying to put out all the fires at once never works. Worse, spending time on a small fire when there is a larger fire raging only hurts the organization.

Letting fires burn is hard to do. Being successful in IT requires a servant mindset focused on making the business and employees successful. That servant mindset makes it very hard to look at a problem that we absolutely know we can help with and say, "I will not deal with that right now because I am working on this other more important problem."

The role of IT leader comes with a wide range of tasks and issues. Attempting to control our time and the demands placed on it is the only way to survive. Reducing interruptions, understanding the flow of the day, and focusing on a smaller number of tasks will help us accomplish more.

Monkeys Everywhere!

A classic Harvard Business Review article, "Management Time: Who's Got the Monkey?" is a great article about how we can make our life miserable if we aren't careful. It is a quick read, but very helpful in framing up how we interact with our team. Monkeys are the various tasks and problems our employees face. The monkey represents the responsibility for the task. We have to feed the monkey with actions and communication. We often (unintentionally) encourage monkeys to jump from the employee's shoulder to our shoulder. This requires us to do the care and feeding of the monkey.

We often encourage monkeys to jump from the employee's shoulder to our shoulder.

I'm not talking about the cute little monkeys that scamper about at the zoo and sit sweetly looking at us. I'm talking about the aggressive, rip the backpack of food from our hands and run away kind. If you have ever visited Gibraltar, you know the kinds of monkeys I'm talking about. You don't want them sitting on your shoulders.

We transfer monkeys to our own shoulder in very subtle ways, and often with the best of intentions. Anytime we say "Let me check into that" or "Send me an email about it," we have allowed the monkey to jump from the employee's shoulders to ours. We now have a brand new, hungry monkey to care for. How many times do we do this in a day or week?

Taking the monkeys has two problems. First is the extra work we signed up for. We have to feed this monkey (work the task) or watch it starve to death, providing a good dose of guilt as we look at yet another task on our plate that we didn't get to. Second, it teaches our teams that they can hand off problems to us. This conflicts with the goal of building a team that stands on its own.

Our team will get a lot more done if they manage their own monkeys — identifying them, feeding them, and releasing them to the wild. (Yeah, the analogy isn't perfect, but stay with me here.) There will always be a few that need to ask questions, but the better equipped our team is to handle them, the fewer the monkeys will jump to our shoulder. More gets done and we can stay focused on managing our own monkeys.

When a team member shows up with a monkey on their shoulder either in our office or email, the monkey immediately starts looking at our shoulder as a nice new place to live. We have one of three choices:

First, we can take the monkey. Now we have a responsibility for the next step in the task. The employee has raised a question or issue about something they are working on and comes to us for help or guidance. It is so easy to come out of this situation with the monkey on our shoulder. *"Let me think about it for a bit." "Send me an email and I'll get back to you." "I'll talk to that person."* All these scenarios end with the monkey joining our already too large menagerie.

Second, we can leave the monkey with the employee. We answer their questions and concerns immediately. In most cases, this is the best solution. It may take more time to talk with the employee about it, but teaching the employee how to deal with it keeps the monkey seated comfortably on their shoulder. And they (the employee, not the monkey) learn how to take better care of future monkeys.

If there is communication that needs to happen, teach the employee how. If a decision needs to be made, ask them what the decision points are and what is important. Add our thoughts into the mix and have them decide. If we have to decide, make it there and then and make sure the employee keeps the monkey.

So we have covered taking the monkey (bad) and leaving the monkey with the employee (good). There is one last option. Make the monkey disappear. Some monkeys are not important enough for us or our employees to keep around. Being ruthless in making monkeys disappear can help everyone stay focused on the important tasks.

When I first learned this analogy, the term was "shoot the monkey" but that disturbs some. Let's consider a magic wand. Wave the wand and poof! the monkey disappears. No more sitting on anyone's shoulder, constantly demanding food. If it helps, imagine the wand sends the monkeys to a happy jungle place where there are no IT shoulders to haunt.

There are always too many monkeys. They are strewn all over our to do lists and many of them are starving to death because of lack of attention. It is better to wave the magic wand to make them go away than to let them die from lack of attention. Or we can just shoot them and put them out of their misery. Your choice.

Constant Decision making

I believe IT leaders have to make the widest variety of decision types. There are all the normal people and company issues other managers face. Then we add IT technology into the mix, with its rapid, always changing environment. And finally, we add consumer technology that is changing how the entire company interacts with technology. This is a tough environment to navigate. The decisions we make daily vary wildly in size and topic. Here are some thoughts, sometimes trivial, sometimes conflicting, about Decision Making in the IT world:

1. Sometimes wrong, never indecisive.

A cute little phrase, perhaps even an exaggeration. Some decisions we need to make today don't have a large impact on the future, or we can easily change them down the road. We shouldn't spend much time to make these decisions. Make the call and go. These types of decisions are also good ones to delegate to the team.

2. Defer where possible.

This option contradicts the one I just mentioned. We never have all the information we want and need when making some decisions. But we don't need to make each decision as soon as we identify it. Sometimes we can defer it to the future. If we have two options and we are putting our budget together, we may not need to decide in order to complete our budget. We could pick the bigger number, or pick an average, and go from there. Deciding later will allow us to have more information.

3. Check with the team.

It is our decision, but asking the team for their opinion can be important. And if the team is not the kind to give their specific recommendation, we can ask them for the criteria for deciding. They might have some insight that we missed.

When someone from the team comes to us for a decision, it may be an excellent opportunity to build trust. Ask them for the criteria and pros and cons. Ask them for their recommendation. If we agree with their assessment and recommendation, they will feel more comfortable making decisions on their own in the future. If we don't agree, we can have a conversation explaining what aspect we put more weight on, and turn it into a teaching moment. And sometimes, the decision is not the one we would make, but it is still a workable decision. Going with the team member's opinion shows trust in them.

4. Make a partial decision.

This one is a combination of deciding fast and deferring. If we can decide part of it now and defer part, we may be ahead. For example, pick a vendor, but don't set the implementation schedule or product options until later.

Some decisions are drivers and some are reactors. Some decisions are tent poles that shape one of those big circus tents. We make other decisions based on the shape of the existing tent. To use another analogy, some decisions are the dog, and some decisions are the tail. The dog always wags the tail, the tail never wags the dog.

Technology decisions are often inadvertent drivers. Changing underlying technology is difficult and can become a driver of other decisions. If we choose not to upgrade our email system, we may not be able to upgrade our call center software. In the Technology part of the book I'll cover some of these issues.

Spend more time on the "dog" decisions and not so much on the "tail" decisions. Just like we manage our time by focusing on the most important tasks, we should focus most of our decision making on the most important decisions. Don't get wrapped up in the small decisions.

> *Some decisions are the dog, and some decisions are the tail. The dog always wags the tail, the tail never wags the dog.*

When we have decided, there are two things to keep in mind. First, don't do the "shoulda coulda woulda" dance. *I should have done this. I could have done that. Decide* with the best information we have at the time and move on. Additional information may come out that would have changed our decision. So it goes. Learn from decisions that didn't work. Beating ourselves up for a decision based on information we didn't or couldn't have had isn't helpful.

Second, we will make mistakes. We will make wrong decisions. In post-decision analysis, it will be clearer when we should have made a different decision. Since we don't have a time machine, we can't go back and change things. Don't hide it or get defensive about it. The best thing to do is to own the mistake, learn from it, and be straight with others. It is hard to do at the beginning, but remember that we are setting a model for others. If our team sees us handling a wrong decision with class and integrity, they will learn and do the same.

Getting good at deciding will set a clearer course for us, the team, and the company. Spend time to get the important decisions right. Try to reduce the time spent deciding on the smaller ones. Learn from mistakes and constantly work to get better.

Walkabouts

The last major point for managing ourselves is this: Stay connected to the organization. As we talked about before, an important part of our job is to understand the business well enough to make good decisions in the IT department. Walkabouts play an important role in this.

If the company is on the Lean journey, production may do Gemba walks. Join them. Listen. Contribute. If you are in a different industry, start taking the long route to and from meetings. Stop by and chat to the person who sent in a Help Desk ticket last week. Start making connections with people you see regularly. There are several benefits.

Asking questions from a place of genuine curiosity usually results in people sharing about their job, what's going well and not so well, and their ideas and opinions.

We learn the physical layout of the buildings and are better able to notice changes. New equipment? New layout? New faces?

Over time, we see the same people and can start conversations. Asking questions from a place of genuine curiosity usually results in people sharing about their job, what's going well and not so well, and their ideas and opinions. Holding the door for someone moving product may allow us to ask questions about the product and where they are taking it.

When the inevitable IT questions pop up, we can turn it into more of a conversation about how they use the systems. What works well, what problems they have and how often they pop up.

If they see us as a friendly face, employees may ask questions about the business. This gives us a sense of what the employees are thinking and feeling. We end up with a better sense of the organization. While not directly impactful on day-to-day IT decisions, we will find ourselves with a deeper understanding of the organization and how it works as an organic entity made up of actual people.

Stop by the desk of someone that put in an IT request and ask a few questions. Since IT requests rarely contain all the information the team will need, there are usually a few questions we can ask. That allows a conversation about their job and challenges. It also allows us to set expectations about when it might get done, especially if it is something that we know will be below a lot of other requests on the priority list.

Another idea is to do one-on-one meetings while walking through the building. While not ideal for private conversations, they can be an excellent way to see the building through the eyes of others. It allows them to see us react to questions that come up and model behavior when, for example, someone asks us to fix their printer.

And people will ask. I don't mind getting asked to fix a printer or some Outlook oddity. If I can't, I'll say so. But I enjoy keeping my fingers on the front lines. I don't know if the head of engineering gets asked to fix a design or if the head of production management gets asked to build parts. I like that it happens in IT.

CHAPTER 17

LEADING THE IT TEAM

Leading IT teams in my career has been challenging and rewarding. I enjoy watching people grow into their position and beyond. I feel satisfaction when a project comes to completion and the organization benefits. Watching a team work together and care about each other is gratifying.

Sure, there are challenges and tough parts and things I would prefer to avoid. It isn't fun working with someone that isn't a good fit for their position, but both the person and the business need to be in a better place, so we do that work. Projects don't always go well. Paperwork and admin tasks are low on the fun scale.

As a leader, our vision heavily influences what the department does, how it behaves, and what its personality is. Our visions for how IT can support the goals of the organization need to meet up with the skills of the team to create a better vision and actual execution of the vision.

In this section, I will cover aspects of leading the IT team:

- Build on their strengths
- Trust the team
- Build a Continuous Improvement culture
- Mistakes Happen — what matters is what happens next.

Build on their strengths

I believe that a core component of leading people is to understand and leverage their strengths. Everyone has parts of their job they are good at and parts they aren't. Knowing the parts they are good at and figuring out how to use that strength is important. Let me give an example.

At a former company, we had an ERP system that would have a data glitch once in a while. These problems often originated in our data, but required a lot of digging to find the problem. Help Desk personnel would go back and forth with the end users trying to track down the problem.

> I believe that a core component of leading people is to understand and leverage their strengths.

On rare occasions, one of the team, Alice, would get pulled into the bad data glitches. She would dive in and figure out the answer quickly. Like a scuba diver surfacing after finding buried treasure, she would triumphantly emerge from her office with the solution and an enormous smile on her face. But it wasn't part of her job, so the Help Desk didn't send them to Alice often.

After a few conversations with the team, I realized not only was Alice good at solving these problems; she was faster than anyone else, better at identifying root cause, and, most importantly, she loved doing it. Finding and resolving that type of problem was very satisfying for her.

So I made the decision that this class of problem was always to go straight to Alice, bypassing the normal help desk process. As a team, we solved this class of problem faster. Alice enjoyed her job more, and the problems became rarer.

Alice had a strength and putting it to use was beneficial to the company, the team, and, of course, Alice.

I have had team members that were great at working with others to resolve process conflicts. Other team members were outstanding at laying out the needed tasks for complicated Change Requests. Still others were great at making sure everyone on the team felt like they belonged. And so forth.

The book *First, Break All The Rules* by Marcus Buckingham and Curt Coffman (Simon & Schuster), was very influential for me early in my management career. It presented the idea, backed up by Gallop Poll business research, that playing to people's strengths was a much more effective management style.

So how should we think about people's strengths? How do we go about discovering them?

The straightforward answer is to watch and listen. Watch what they do at work and see where their enthusiasm pops out. Listen to their answer to "How's it going?" to see what things they talk about.

I found that specific questions can get to the core. For example:

"Imagine a great day at work. You feel accomplished. You feel good about what you did today. You really like your job. What did you do?"

"When you are getting ready to come to work in the morning, what do you hope that you will get to work on?"

Listen carefully to the answers. Tease out the specifics. For example, I often hear "I like to solve problems." Follow up with questions to understand the kind of problems, the kind of solutions, what part of the business, or how they solved them. Over time, each person will reveal what they like doing and what they are good at.

We need to ask ourselves these questions as well. As a leader, it is very important to understand what we are good at and what we aren't. Imagine the end of an upbeat movie where the main character is triumphant. What happens at work to make us feel that way? What is it we did that makes us feel that accomplished?

If we never feel that way, we might want to look closely at our job. It might not be a great fit. That's true for the team as well. Not everyone is a "jump up and down with happiness" kind of person, but everyone should at least have moments in their job where they feel satisfaction for a task well done. Sometimes we have to listen to the complaints and understand the parts of their job where they feel underappreciated. Maybe that is part of their strength and we haven't set up the job to give them that satisfaction.

It isn't possible for any of us to spend every day only doing things that make us feel awesome. That's why they call it work. Every job has parts of it that don't thrill us, and maybe even some parts that we actively dislike.

But if we understand what parts make each person feel better about themselves and their job, we can make changes, some subtle, some overt, to leverage their strengths. This results in a stronger department and an increase in job satisfaction and engagement.

Trust the team

As leaders, we set the overall direction of the team. Making sure there is a consistent philosophy and culture is hard. And important. By setting the right philosophies about how to think about the work in front of them, they will make better decisions. Here are some examples of philosophies and culture:

- Does the team understand when to take the harder long-term path and when to implement something quick and dirty?
- Does the team know how to identify all the stakeholders for a problem? Or do they always ask for the list? Do they want to learn who the right people are?
- Does the team recognize riskier situations and act accordingly? Even better, do they recognize future risks and take actions to reduce those?
- Does the team manage expectations for those waiting for tasks to complete?

We need to look into the mirror hard on this next part. It may very well be the hardest part to building trust with our team. When (not if!) our employee solves a problem, writes a memo, or decides differently from what we would do, what is our reaction? If our reaction is to overrule the employee or redo the work, then we are doing it wrong. While there may be times when this is necessary, we need to ask ourself if their decision will get the same result. It will never be precisely the same result, but if, at a high level, it meets the requirements and gets the job done; we need to shut up and let their work ride.

If we are constantly criticizing how they do tasks, they ask us to review more. If they feel that we are going to override their decisions, they will check with us more. When that happens, we have created a monkey zoo in our office and we won't get anything done.

The first time we swallow our words and accept something different from what we would have done is the first time we trust our team. The employee will see that and feel empowered to do it again. And maybe, just maybe, we learn that our way isn't always the best.

That doesn't mean that we can't have discussions about what is important and why it is important. For instance, if they implement a change that misses a longer-term point, say not considering an upcoming infrastructure change, asking a few questions first to see if they have thought about it is better than pointing out how we would have done it. They may have thought about it and solved it a different way.

> *The first time we swallow our words and accept something different from what we would have done is the first time we trust our team.*

Yes, there is a chance that it will blow up in our faces. And we will feel embarrassed because we didn't keep a close enough eye on things. But we need to stay focused on the larger prize: if we have a team that we can trust and that runs hard, our department will get more done than if we need to be in the loop on everything.

People have an internal drive that will push them forward. How much they drive forward depends on many things: their skills, knowledge of the organization, knowledge about what we expect of them, and self-confidence. The employee that pushes forward on their own is valuable and can overcome missing skills. I would rather steer someone than to have to push them. I would rather have someone who makes mistakes from time to time because they are running too fast than to have someone hesitant to step out of their little area. Especially if they learn from their mistakes. I believe that, in the end, the organization will get more done with people who drive themselves than people I need to push.

I hope that I have given a starting point for trusting employees more. Start small, communicate philosophies, let them be different. It is ok if we don't know exactly what our team is working on today or where something is in the priority list. Being able to trust that they are working on the right things goes a long way.

I got a letter recently into "Ask the IT Director" that illustrates more about this issue. Here is the letter and answer reprinted.

Dear IT Director,

I am a new manager. My team keeps coming to me with questions. They seem unable to make decisions on their own. I have too many of their tasks on my plate, and I can't get it all done without working 16-hour days and weekends. Help!

Drowning in Delano

Dear Drowning,

Ouch, sounds like you are paying the price for a prior manager that didn't trust their team. Changing behavior like that is hard. You need to trust that they can do the job you expect of them, and they need to trust you to provide them useful advice and guidance. The bottom line is that you are starting from scratch on the trust game.

You are the one that needs to take the first step. Read the Harvard Business Review article, "Management Time: Who's Got the Monkey?" Your staff walks into your office with monkeys and leaves with empty shoulders. You end up with lots of monkeys that aren't yours. Many of them will starve. Even if you work long hours and take work home.

Get your staff to take care of their own monkeys. They need to understand that they are responsible for feeding, training, and ultimately releasing each of their monkeys. The monkeys can't take a detour through your office. It starts with you politely, but firmly refusing to take their monkeys.

When employees come into your office with the full intention to hand you a monkey, don't let them. If they give you several choices, ask them which option they think is the best and why. Ask a few questions to point out areas for consideration. If they know the answer, great. If they don't, the monkey is still on their shoulder while they figure it out.

Silence is your friend here. Silence isn't something that you need to fill. Ask your question and wait. If they come back with a quick "I don't know," you will need to push back a bit to get them to think. Maybe you can ask, "How would you figure it out?" or "What are some issues here?"

Often, you can build on the answers they provide. "That's a good point. Here are some other things to think about." Try to avoid the "No, that's wrong" answer. Nothing kills initiative faster than asking them for a recommendation and then telling them they are wrong. It is a teaching moment, so build on where they start from.

If they are missing some important pieces, teach them. What important factor are they missing? Or maybe they aren't missing it but have a different opinion on its importance. Ask them if they have considered this factor or that issue. Explain why you think one aspect is more important than another. Encourage them to disagree with you and make them explain why. Talk about risk in the decision.

If they are heading towards an acceptable answer, encourage them. Note that word. "Acceptable." Most of the decisions at this level have multiple answers that can be successful. Your way is not the only way. It may not even be the best way. Let them make the call. Clarify that it is their decision and you support them.

And this is the hard part for you, Drowning in Delano. Are there decisions you can delegate because they are low risk and because your team knows what is important? Of course there are. Let them make those decisions and support them. Otherwise, you end up in the situation where they come to you to find out your right answer.

Conversely, if you are searching out monkeys to take, then you are really doing it wrong. Don't stick your nose in unless you feel it is very important.

Here is one more analogy: coaching sports. Soccer (football for my World readers) coaches do most of their work during practice sessions and don't call out plays during a game. Watch a top tier professional soccer match. Very few coaches yell and scream from the sidelines. They have trained their team to deal with what they will face in the game. American football coaches, on the other hand, call each play on both offense and defense.

(Excuse me a moment, while I talk to the serious sports fans in the back for a moment. Yes, I know it isn't the same and that each sport is different. "Analogy" doesn't mean "is exactly the same in all aspects." Your sport is awesome and an excellent example of some of the most physically demanding and skilled play on the planet.)

Management in the business world should aim to be more like the soccer coaches. While there aren't practices and games, working with your employees so they can manage the day-to-day decisions and actions more on their own will help them, and you, be more productive.

One last check on how you are doing in this process. What happens when you go on vacation? Is there an enormous pile of questions and decisions waiting for you when you return? Or have they managed their work in your absence? Work towards that and your team will thrive more, and you will have more time on your hands.

Good Luck,

The IT Director

Build a continuous improvement culture

The odds of being successful go up if there is continuous improvement built into the company culture. This applies across the company, each department, and each person. The need to get better especially applies to IT. An IT department that isn't improving is like all those mac&cheese meals we had when we first moved out on our own. Tasty, but eventually boring and unsatisfying.

How do we build continuous improvement into our IT department? It is as much about attitude as it is about training or technology. Ideally, each member of our team wants to get better, wants to make the team better, and wants to make the company better. How do we encourage that?

I suggest coming at this from two angles: the personal and the process.

Let's start with the personal. In one-on-ones with team members, there should always be a few minutes spent talking about learning and improving. Make it part of the regular conversation. Each person should have one thing (only one — remember Focus & Finish) they are trying to get better at.

Don't make this primarily about improving a weakness. If there is something significant that needs fixing, by all means, work with them to get it fixed. Most of the time, though, they are motivated to improve in an area that interests them and builds on their strengths. Do they thrive on learning new technology? Do they wish they were better at a soft skill? Frame these as part of the continuous improvement.

Improving processes provides a counter to the personal improvements. If they are having conversations about improving themselves and having conversations about improving process, they will think about continuous improvement often. That will build it into the culture.

> *Positive feedback is critical for driving any change.*

We have several processes in IT. Help Desk tickets, projects, financial, change control, etc. Pick one and work with the team to improve it. The conversation should identify a couple of shortcomings. Have the team come up with ideas for improvement, choose one, and implement. Give kudos to the ones with the ideas and the ones that implemented it. Positive feedback is critical for driving any change.

Make these process improvements part of team meetings and communications. Keep them visible.

If our company has a corporate Continuous Improvement program, make sure IT is a strong partner in it. Use the tools and processes provided.

Not everyone will have the same enthusiasm for this. However, if we can build on some small successes, others will see the value and start contributing.

Learning

Let's dive a little more into the learning part of continuous improvement. While applicable to the entire company, technological changes make learning especially critical for IT.

New technologies aimed at businesses arrive daily. Even something as common as Windows servers will regularly get additional features and will be outdated in just a few years if not upgraded. Whole swaths of our central IT architecture will have something newer and better available in the marketplace. We will probably have one or two major upgrades each year.

Complicating that is the fact that consumer technology is changing faster than the drummer for Spinal Tap. New phones, apps, and form factors are influencing our user base. The employees in our organizations are becoming more knowledgeable and capable of using technology. Shadow IT is becoming easier to build and harder to influence.

The IT Department stands in the middle of this technology hurricane. Learn enough to decide what to implement. Learn enough about what we implement to support it effectively. Some will run projects. Others will need to learn enough about it to educate and support the rest of the company.

As the IT leader, we need to understand where everyone on the team sits on these questions:

- Can they quickly understand how new technologies work?
- Do they understand the business enough to determine if we can apply the technology to problems and improvements?
- Do they understand enough about the current technology portfolio so they recognize how something new might fit in?

None of those questions are actually about the technology itself. They do, however, have a large impact on how well we can bring in new technology. Building the above skills in the team just puts them in a better position for the continual learning they need to do.

Our team also brings their own biases to the mix. For example, the employee that sees a shiny object in every new technology, or, conversely, the employee that only sees problems. Sometimes, we have an employee that knows one technology and isn't interested in learning others.

The team will also change over time. New employees will come in and need to learn the technology in place. Regardless of the experience they have, rarely do they have deep knowledge of all the pieces in use.

They will also need to learn multiple technologies because we likely don't have a big enough staff to have one person per major system. At the very least, we will need to have a backup person for each system.

Organizations usually have a central system, such as an ERP system, which plays an outsized role in the team's learning. Unless our company is just using the ERP system as a point solution, only doing one thing with no thoughts to expanding, there will be a constant drive to learn about new nooks and crannies.

Fortunately, most ERP systems have a design, a feel, a style that, once we understand it, makes learning new functionality easier. We may need to learn a new module that the company hasn't used before, but if we have a solid understanding of how the ERP system is built, we will already know how to navigate, search, create, and report on the information.

So how do we deal with all the learning that needs to happen? How do we keep the team in a position to support the technologies the company uses today and tomorrow? Here are a few ways:

- Let's start with the obvious one: videos on the internet. Vendors and users will probably have tutorial videos available for free. Check all the common web sites.

- Use vendor training where available. There seems to be a trend towards more online training and fewer in person sessions, especially from smaller technology companies. Leverage what is available. Vendor user groups or online forums are also an excellent source of information.

- Online communities are available for most technologies. Be active in the ones that matter.

- Use the test system as a playground for employees to try out parts of the system they may not be familiar with. Use it to get them over their fear of breaking something.

- Work to share knowledge within the team. Have someone with experience create a short, high-level explanation of the system.

Have the team add troubleshooting information as time goes by. If the sharing is part of their regular activities, it will become second nature.

- Share best practices with similar companies. Find them, make the contacts, and then explore commonalities and differences. I've had luck getting entire IT staffs together to compare notes. Or maybe just the applications or infrastructure teams. In these joint company settings, we can find comfort and knowledge in others' experiencing similar problems and frustrations with tech, vendors, and employees. Have a few larger topics to start the conversation and they will take it from there. Sharing experiences and problems will take place naturally.

- Find organizations that connect IT departments. These groups will connect the team with others doing similar work. There are at least two strong no-vendor peer groups in my part of the country, and one of them is nationwide.

Mistakes happen — what matters is what happens next

Imagine two scenarios.

First, we are at a restaurant. Scanning the menu, we see lots of great options. It's hard to decide. But finally, we do. We put our order in and sit back, mouth watering in anticipation. Finally, it arrives. And it's wrong. We wanted french fries and got brussels sprouts. Or vice versa. Either way, it disappoints us. When we point it out, the restaurant is very apologetic, brings out new food and takes something off the bill.

Second scenario. Same restaurant. Same menu. And we once again get the brussels sprouts. Sigh. This time, the restaurant suggests that we really do want the brussels sprouts because they are superb. They seem reluctant to fix the problem. Finally, they bring out a small plate of fries, giving the impression that it is a big hassle. And make no change to the bill.

Leaving aside the brutal reality of restaurant economics, the first scenario is better. The restaurant made a mistake, but they acknowledged it and fixed it quickly.

We all have stories like this: a car takes too long to get repaired, a movie theater charges an extra ticket on the credit card, or a vendor drops the ball on a task handoff. A mistake is made and then handled. Sometimes we discover it. Sometimes, even better, the provider discovers it and tells us about it. *"I'm sorry, but it will take a day longer to get your car done. We ordered the wrong part. We discovered it, ordered the correct part, and we have taken 5% off your bill for the delay."*

When someone acknowledges their mistakes and works to make amends, we feel differently about them. Sometimes, these situations bring a vendor and Customer closer together because we have now seen how they do business and what level of integrity they have. Everybody makes mistakes, some handle it better.

At our work in the IT department, we are the provider. We are the restaurant, the auto repair shop, the movie theater. While we may not call them 'customers', we must build a strong customer service mentality. We will make mistakes. How we deal with them is the important part.

There are two parts to "dealing with" a mistake: Acknowledgment and Improving.

(1) Acknowledgment

Acknowledging mistakes is important. It lets the other person know that we are transparent in how things are working. They know something is wrong, so don't hide it.

If we drop the ball on something, apologize. Owning the mistake makes it clear that we are not trying to cover things up.

Now there is a gray area between trumpeting our team's mistakes from the tallest tower and hiding them. We will make mistakes we don't need to broadcast. Broadcasting differs from acknowledging them. Acknowledging them to those directly involved is key here.

Having a reputation for not owning up to mistakes will undermine our credibility in the organization. Much better to have a reputation for owning and fixing our mistakes.

Acknowledging a mistake allows everyone to move on. When there are arguments about whom to blame, the entire organization suffers.

(2) Improving

We can't really give a $10 coupon when IT makes a mistake. We can't give them a meal at half price. But we can reduce the chance of making that mistake again. It isn't possible to prevent all future mistakes, but communicating that we are working to reduce mistakes makes a lot of difference.

Internally, the focus should be on the future. Do we need to prevent this mistake from happening? Or do we need to reduce the possibility that it will happen? Risk analysis and mitigation (chapter 4) can help here.

Mistakes come from the process more than the person: a process that doesn't take a certain situation into account, or a person we haven't trained sufficiently. That doesn't mean we don't individually mess up, but it means that improving the process is more beneficial than placing blame.

Mistakes can be teaching moments. Often, a self-driven person will see the mistake they made and come up with a suitable response to reduce the chance of it happening in the future. Sometimes, though, it is helpful to talk about the bigger picture behind the problem.

For example, if they dropped the ball on a task because they had too many active tasks at once, the conversation shouldn't be about dropping the ball, but about how to better manage open tasks and the need to focus and finish to avoid these kinds of problems.

Yes, sometimes an employee makes too many mistakes, and there is a mismatch between the needs of the job and their skills that we need to address. But this isn't a common thing.

It is far more common that we all make mistakes. When they happen, we need to acknowledge it, learn from it, and move on.

Staff Training

Bringing in new technology requires our team to learn how to support it and to help the organization use it. We need to understand that this learning takes a big effort.

When adding new technology to our portfolio, does our staff already know something like it? For example, replacing one vendor's network gear with another vendor's gear may be a smaller effort if it uses a similar command set.

We need to understand the expectations for the ongoing support role IT will play. These expectations come from the organization and from the team, and will lead directly to a level of training that IT needs.

The simplest way to think about this is as a solid box/glass box. IT takes care of installing the product, doing initial setup, and is responsible for backups and security (solid box). The business learns how to integrate the product into their business processes (glass box).

The term "solid box" comes from the testing world. The tester only sees the outside of the product and knows nothing about how the inside works.

In a solid box scenario, IT sees the product from the outside and doesn't need to interact or understand how it works. Imagine installing a piece of specialty software, say a statistics package, on an employee's computer. The IT person does the install and knows how to start the software, but doesn't understand statistics and doesn't know how to use the program. That is up to the employee to figure out.

In a multi-user product, IT gets more involved in the internals, perhaps knowing how to do some basic configuration and user management. If that is all we do, we still consider this a solid box scenario.

The term "glass box" also comes from testing. In glass box testing, the tester knows how the product works on the inside. In the glass box support scenario, IT knows the inside of the product and provides support. An example would typically be the email system where IT handles all the administration functions, but also gets involved in the internals of the email client, supporting email and calendar functionality. ERP systems are also good examples of places we expect our teams to understand how things work inside the product at some level.

Glass box support has a higher level of required IT training. When considering a new system, the decision of a solid box or glass box support should be an intentional one.

There is a trap out there that we need to be careful of. Consider the situation where a member of IT runs the initial implementation of an intended solid box scenario. Because the IT person is good, they will learn some internals of the system. Because they are in IT and have experience learning how these products work, they may learn the internals (glass box) faster than the users and end up being an unintended support resource that the users rely on.

It worked like this at one company. They were replacing their Learning Management System (LMS). The existing system was old and wasn't being updated. We put a team together, including an IT representative, to do the selection. The team selected the new system. This system was a cloud-based service that would interface with other internal systems (user accounts, ERP, data warehouse).

The IT representative became the project manager (IT-PM). Over the course of the implementation, the IT-PM sat in on all the training from the vendor and learned the interfaces, eventually become knowledgeable about the internals of the system.

Others on the team learned that they could go to the IT-PM to get answers to internal "how does this work?" type of questions. Any problem with the internal workings of the system went to the IT-PM. The original goal had been a solid box situation, with the training department becoming the expert on the system, but the particular skills and work ethic of the IT-PM created a glass box situation.

The IT-PM wanted to make sure the project was successful and answered all questions. If she came across a problem, she figured it out.

After the team implemented the system, the Training department and other users continued to ask her questions. Since she was conscientious and helpful, she did her best to answer them.

Then she moved to a new role.

The company had built an expectation that there would be an expert in the LMS system in the IT department. Because they hadn't built their own expertise on the internals, we had created an unhealthy dependency that added limited value to the business.

It took about a year for the training department to build up the expertise to answer all the support questions. If they hadn't depended on IT, they wouldn't have had that year gap.

To summarize, in the name of "good service to the business," the IT person became an expert beyond what we expected. While this was helpful during the implementation, it became a responsibility in IT for much longer than it should have. The business didn't know the system, so couldn't move forward with it as fast as they wanted to.

In this chapter, we covered some aspects of leading an IT team. Now let's move on to building that team.

CHAPTER 18

BUILDING THE RIGHT TEAM

Getting the right people on our teams is difficult. Each person's skills and personality will affect the team dynamics. Those of us with years of experience have seen different teams with distinct personalities. The dynamics of the team make a difference in its effectiveness.

Not that everyone needs to be best friends before we can have an excellent team. Whether they hang out for beers after work doesn't have much impact on their effectiveness. But they will have to work together. In the department that has to deal with more technology than any other department in the company, it is critical that our teams work well together.

Working well together doesn't mean that everyone needs to be the same. Like plywood made of thin sheets of wood with different orientations, a team is stronger when the parts are not all the same.

Like plywood made of thin sheets of wood with different orientations, a team is stronger when the parts are not all the same.

Keep this in mind when hiring. It won't take long into our managing career before we get to hire someone. This section presents some things to think about when building our teams, specifically around interviewing.

First, we have to cover the basics. Putting the time in to create an appropriate job description is not one of my favorite tasks, but it is worth the effort. Be clear on what skills the candidate must have (required) and what skills they should have (preferred).

This can be tricky. Keep required skills and experience minimal. If we truly require a skill, then don't waste time interviewing candidates who don't have it. This seems obvious, but I have seen situations where an awesome candidate didn't meet a particular requirement, but the right move was to hire them. College degrees fall into this category, which has led me to use phrasing such as "college degree or equivalent experience required."

Next, put time into interview questions to determine if they have the needed skills and attributes. Asking the same set of questions to each candidate allows for easier comparison. Follow-up questions are, of course, different for each candidate. Starting with common questions and diving into each candidate's specifics makes it easier to determine who should move forward.

And it isn't just about questions. Use exercises to allow the candidate to show their skills. I found that adding exercises to the second-round interviews gives a better picture of the candidate's skills.

Finally, remember we all get nervous when we are in interviews. We want to make a good impression and we worry about making mistakes or doing poorly. Putting the candidate at ease early on will help their true personality come out. I don't subscribe to the school of thought that says we should make the interview a difficult, tortuous affair. That style may work for some, but that isn't the kind of team I want to build, so it isn't the kind of interview I want to hold. Challenging, thoughtful, hard, yes. Tortuous, no.

So we have an appropriate job description and some questions and exercises that get at the hard skills of the job. Now, let's look at some soft skills that can help us.

Self-Motivated

Self-motivated people will get more done in the long run with less work on our part. As we talked about in the prior chapter, we want to give our team high level priorities and let them drive them forward. Having an employee that needs constant pushing is not a good fit.

Ask questions that will allow the candidate to give examples of initiative. In the interview, asking good follow-up questions, including other examples, is important to get a deeper understanding of the candidate.

Example Questions:

- Tell me about a time where you had to make a decision when your supervisor was not around.
- Tell me about a project or improvement you suggested that was implemented.
- Tell me how you manage a To Do list that is longer than you can get done that day.
- Tell me about a job where you had a lot of flexibility in prioritizing your tasks. How did you decide what order to work on things?

These questions will give us a sense of what kinds of things the candidate will do on their own. Have they pushed an idea into reality? Are they comfortable in situations where they create and manage their To Do list every day? How do they manage the normal IT situation of more work than time?

Technically Strong

This means two things: the technology they know and the technology they can learn. Change is a constant in IT, and there will always be new technology to learn.

Example Questions:

- Teach me something technical.

- Tell me about the last time that you had to come up to speed on a new technology.
- How do you learn new technical information?
- Pick a large system that you know well. Describe an intermittent problem and how you tracked it down.

It is important in these questions to ask follow-up questions to understand how the candidate learns.

I use exercises in many of my interviews. Help Desk candidates have to fix a computer and install software. Business Analysts have to interview someone to write up the requirements for a small project. Developers have to write code. I have candidates give a 15-minute training to us to see how they communicate information.

I recently started providing candidates with some information about our systems and then asked them questions about it. Not to see if they memorized it (the interview is open book), but to see how much they can build on what I provided. Can they only recite back what I wrote or can they understand the implications of the technology? This is especially useful when looking for an experienced candidate.

For example, we provide candidates with an explanation of one of our software building blocks and then ask questions about how the tool might be used and what potential problems there might be. It doesn't matter that they don't know our technology environment or business. Strong candidates quickly learn the material and understand the implications.

Sense of Humor

Finding someone that enjoys life and can find the fun in the workday will help those tough days when things aren't going well. Working in IT can frustrate and sometimes be unrewarding. Seeing the humor in life makes it easier.

Remember that everyone's sense of humor is different. There is no correct sense of humor. Also, remember that Scalzi's Law (https://whatever.scalzi.com/2010/06/16/the-failure-state-of-clever/) is a true and valid thing.

Humor is hard to determine in an interview. Sometimes the informal chit-chat at the beginning and end of the interview can give us a sense of things, although interviews bring out the safe behavior in people.

I use the pre-interview chit-chat to show that it is ok to show a bit of humor. Keep the humor at word play or self-deprecating comments. Do not aim the humor at others.

When describing our organizations to a candidate, include positive words (fun? laughs? etc.) when appropriate. Even if a candidate doesn't ask, they will want to know what kind of personality our team has.

Willing to Help

Everyone gets stumped at some point. If team members know they can reach out for help, they will get unstuck faster. Conversely, if they will help constructively, others will see them as a resource.

We want employees that provide help in a teaching or mentoring way. Taking over the task and just doing it may not be the best response. Sometimes it is a capacity problem ("I can't finish these three tasks by tomorrow.") and taking on the task is appropriate. But often providing ideas, suggestions, or quick research, can be helpful in getting someone unstuck.

And if people go to someone for help, get the help, and learn something, well, that is a win/win.

Example Questions:

- Tell us about a time where you helped someone on your team.
- Tell us about a team that was very successful on a project. What was your role?
- Tell us about a project that failed. What happened? Is there anything you could have done differently?

If we listen carefully, we will hear bits and pieces of how they work with others. Even a candidate interviewing for their very first job should have some examples of helping others.

Use this to build a sense of how the candidate will contribute to the team.

Communication Skills

This is a stinker. Everyone wants every team member to have exceptional communication skills. But what does that mean? Communication, at its core, means that a message moves from one person's brain to another. It is inherently a two-person task, a sender and a receiver. Having someone who writes well or speaks well is only part of the goal. We want to hire someone who understands their audience, tailors the message to them, and verifies the other person received the message.

Another factor is communicating to a single person and communicating to a larger group. Whether written or verbal, communicating to a group needs to take the attributes of the group into account. I can tailor a message if I am talking to one person. If I am communicating to a group, I need to take the entire group into account and make tradeoffs on how I communicate.

In the interview, consider having the candidate teach something technical to a group. Pull in others from IT to create an audience, but also consider pulling people from outside IT. I allow the topic to be anything that the candidate knows really well, preferably work related.

Consider not telling the candidate much about the group they are presenting to. See if they ask for introductions to learn their audience.

Another possibility is to have a bit of homework for the second-round interview. For example, have the candidate write up a one-page introduction to a system they know well directed at non-IT management in their company. The purpose is to explain, from the organization's point of view, what the system does and a bit about how it works. We set the exercise up to force the writer to distill the system down significantly. It is important to see how they organize their thoughts and communicate the basics of the system. It also shows how well they understand the business they are working at.

For help desk candidates, we put actual tickets in front of the candidate. We can learn about their technical knowledge and about how they communicate with end users.

Business Awareness

IT does not exist in a vacuum. The more each person understands the business, the better day-to-day decisions they will make. The required depth of their knowledge depends on the job role.

There are some basics that everyone should know, at least at a high level. What kind of business is the organization in? Who are the Customers? What kinds of employees are there? What are the major parts of the company?

The Help Desk may not know the larger business processes, but they should learn how individuals fit into the mix. When helping someone, ask questions. Many people like talking about their job and appreciate when people express interest. For example, after fixing a printer, ask a chitchat-type question about what they print and what they use it for. Show genuine interest in the person and how they contribute to the company's success.

Each role in IT will think of the business differently. Infrastructure will think about where people sit, what kinds of data and systems they interact with, what security issues a group has, how much storage, what kinds of files are they storing, and moving data around.

The applications team will focus on the business processes. They will spend a larger portion of their day working with different departments, learning how the pieces of the company fit together.

What we want to find out during the interview is their interest and ability to learn about our organization.

Example Questions:

- During the resume review (typically the first part of the interview), ask what their prior employers do. Ask follow-ups to understand what level of detail they know.

- If they worked at a manufacturing company, ask how often they were out on the production floor.
- What kinds of company improvement projects were happening at a prior company? Were you ever involved in one of them?
- Have you been able to interact with Customers at any of your jobs?

The above list is a supplement to the normal questions aimed at determining skills and experience. Hiring a new member for our team is an important part of our job, and trying to figure it out during a set of interviews is a challenge. The above topics and questions can help, but we have to work to get better at it.

One last note on hiring. Each person who submits a resume is a real live person with hopes and dreams. A friend of mine told me she reminds herself of that each time she sits down to review a stack of resumes. When going through dozens of resumes at a time, this is easy to forget.

Each person who submits a resume is a real live person with hopes and dreams.

A few years ago, I had the misfortune of job hunting twice in one year because of acquisitions and layoffs. A frustrating number of companies sent the automated "thanks for your resume" email, and then I heard nothing again. Not even a form email saying "thanks but no thanks." As a job applicant, I didn't know where I stood. I didn't have a problem being rejected; I had a problem with not hearing anything. Why are HR departments ghosting candidates?

Talking with others, this seems to be a common practice. One of my interns kept track of his job applications and found that over half of the companies did not respond after the immediate "thanks for your resume" auto-response. These companies ghosted him more than half the time. Ghosting applicants is rude and unprofessional.

Especially when it is unnecessary. Most companies larger than startups use online job application systems. These systems provide simple ways to send emails to groups of candidates. All rejected candidates should get a response. Write the generic response once, then set up the system to respond to everyone that doesn't make the cut. Leaving them wondering is not a respectful way to treat people applying to our company.

Candidates for positions on our teams deserve better than that.

Spiders & Conductors

There are many excellent books and articles about leadership; read some of them. There is no right model of leadership, so read widely. This section covers something I noticed long ago about leadership styles, which I haven't seen in any book.

First, let's review the basics. A leader is one who leads people, gets them to all go in the same direction, encourages them to care about the work they do. A leader explains the rules, processes, and priorities. Strong leaders have a worldview that imprints on their team. And each leader has a style that influences the behavior of the organization.

> *I believe that both leadership styles are necessary in a company.*

I propose those styles fall into two types: Spiders & Conductors. Spiders create a web of tight connections between themselves and others. Conductors coordinate the independent work of others, like the conductor of an orchestra.

When I first started thinking about this dichotomy, I believed that one was better than the other. Over time, I have seen that there is value in each. They have different strengths and weaknesses and an organization with just Spiders or just Conductors would struggle. This deepened my belief that both leadership styles are necessary in a company.

Understanding Spiders and Conductors also taught me that leadership styles, while innate, can adjust depending on the situation. Not very much, but enough to be successful in a wider variety of situations. For example, we may realize that one team needs more direct attention, and another team can operate more independently.

So let's look at the two types in more detail to understand their impact on our organization.

Spiders

The first type of leader is a "Spider." Spiders are often very good at motivating individuals at a personal level. They build strong connections with their team. Spiders work closely with individuals to make sure that each team member understands what they expect and how things should work. Spiders take pride in answering all questions that arise. There is often a stream of people in and out of their offices.

Spiders create a web of connections in their department and organization. A Spider sits in the middle of the web, working all the threads to make sure the team achieves its goals. All threads lead to the Spider.

Spiders know an immense amount about their area of the organization. They know the people, processes, and data in great detail. They can tell us the status of all the projects in their area, and who is doing what task next.

> Spiders know an immense amount about their area of the organization. They know the people, processes, and data in great detail.

Spiders can often appear overworked, as they have their hands in everything. They can become a bottleneck as many decisions and actions go through them.

Spiders can drive change quickly through their organization by working with each person to make sure they understand the required processes and actions. Because they are deeply connected to each person, Spiders know how to talk to each person to make sure they understand the change. Because the Spider is so involved in the day-to-day workings of each member of the team, the Spider can enforce the new behavior.

Conductors

The other type of leader is a "Conductor." Think of a conductor standing in front of an orchestra. The conductor runs rehearsals and leads the performance. The

conductor knows the music deeply. The conductor knows how all the distinct parts of the orchestra fit together. How they should sound when everything is right. What to change and tweak when groups aren't working well together. It is common for a guest conductor to step in for just a few rehearsals and lead a successful concert.

The conductor of an orchestra gives overall signals, cueing timing and pacing. A Conductor in an organization understands how the overall business runs, how processes move between departments, and what affects the pacing and speed of the company. They make adjustments in the department as needed.

A Conductor in an organization understands how the overall business runs, how processes move between departments, and what affects the pacing and speed of the company.

The Conductor builds an environment where everyone understands a common vision, everyone knows their job well, and everyone can work for themselves. The Conductor describes the results and then leaves the team to figure out how to deliver it.

This is not always easy. The Conductor needs to teach prioritization and the larger view to the team members so they can operate more effectively. Some team members won't understand the larger picture. In these cases, the Conductor may need to become a little more Spider-ish.

The Conductor understands the interfaces between the groups and can communicate effectively to each group to build a better ensemble. She understands the strengths of each group and can adjust to play off those strengths.

A Conductor is more likely to respond to a question from a team member with another question. *What do you think? What options have you considered?* Conductors want team members to answer the question themselves next time.

Conductors can identify and communicate larger organizational changes. They can paint the picture of what the organization needs to be, making it easier for everyone to understand.

Compare & Contrast

To better illustrate the strengths and weaknesses of these two styles, let's look at individual points. We may perceive some of these as good or bad, but it depends on the situation. As I mentioned before, our company needs both leadership styles.

Spiders connect with individuals. Conductors connect with groups. Spiders know how individuals should work together. Conductors know how groups should work together.

> *Spiders connect with individuals. Conductors connect with groups. Spiders know how individuals should work together. Conductors know how groups should work together.*

Leaders will eventually leave their positions. When Spiders leave, they leave a vacancy in the team's day-to-day operations. A team can feel lost during the vacancy. Momentum will help, but they are used to the spider making many of the decisions. The personal connections the Spider has will increase the sense of loss. When a Conductor leaves, there is less of a short-term impact. The teams are used to operating independently and don't need the Conductor as much for day to day. The longer-term impact of a Conductor leaving will show up as time goes by and the groups get out of sync.

Spiders believe that today and tomorrow are most important. The future will take care of itself if we get today right. Conductors believe that the future is inevitable and we need to plan it. Get the future right and today will take care of itself.

Both Spiders and Conductors know the people on their teams. Both know how to get excellent performance out of their teams.

Spiders work closely with each individual to make sure they are both doing the right things *and* doing things right. Conductors won't be as close on the day-to-day tasks but will better know how the team interacts with the rest of the organization. The Conductor presumes her team is competent and able to do their job.

Conductors talk more about priorities and processes. Spiders talk more about tasks and next steps. Conductors can get frustrated when the people don't understand the bigger picture. Spiders get frustrated when one of their team is an independent operator and doesn't want to check in as frequently as the Spider wants.

Because the Spider makes many of the decisions and is involved closely in the day-to-day activities, rarely does someone do something too far from what the Spider wants. Because the Conductor provides direction and priorities, but leaves decisions more to the individual, the team may execute tasks differently than the Conductor might expect. If the outcome is what the Conductor wants, great. If not, the Conductor may struggle to resolve the situation.

Developing Future Leaders

Outstanding leaders are always looking for other leaders. If we have a strong team, there will be at least one or two that have leadership potential. They have become a leader among peers in the team. People look to them for opinions. The team accepts their suggestions frequently.

> *Outstanding leaders are always looking for other leaders.*

They probably show spider or conductor tendencies in how they operate today. When they talk about the rest of the company, do they give details about the people (spider) or do they talk about how the disparate groups work together (conductor)?

Developing a leader requires that we give them additional responsibility at some point. Projects with lots of tasks and people will interest the Spiders. Projects with a larger impact across the organization will interest Conductors.

Future leaders will first become a leader among peers and will be an influence on the team beyond what we might expect of someone of their experience. Both Spiders and Conductors will benefit from being the interface with other groups, but approach the task differently. Spiders can tell us all about the individuals in the group and the processes they follow. Conductors can tell us how that group fits into the larger picture and how the organization influences them.

Spiders and Conductors are different types of leaders. They bring unique sets of skills and understanding to their position and will manage people in different ways. Our organizations need both types. Our own leadership style will lean towards one type or the other. Understanding the strengths and limitations of each type can help us become a better leader.

Contractors and Consultants

We saw this diagram back in Business & IT (chapter 8).

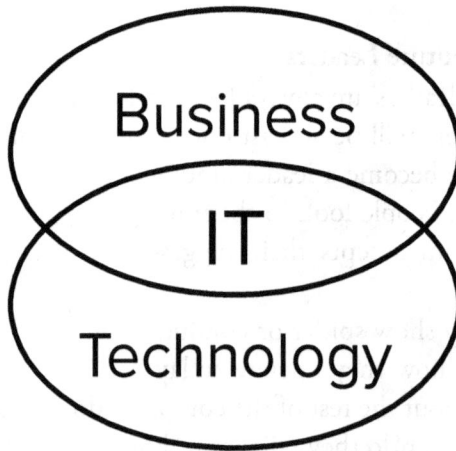

As we lead our teams, sometimes we need more expertise or capacity than we have. In the diagram, think of this as moving away from the overlap where IT lives. If we need deeper business knowledge, we talk to others from the business. Unfortunately, we can't do that for technology. If we need expertise or capacity, we have to go outside the business. Used properly, we can leverage contractors and consultants to accomplish more.

In my experience, it is difficult to run an IT department and never use an outside contractor or consultant. The technology world is too complex and dynamic to know everything internally. The demands of various technologies differ wildly, and the learning curves for some are very large.

While the definitions vary, I use the following:

- *Contractors* can be useful when we need to augment our staff. Maybe we lose a person and need coverage while we hire a replacement. Maybe we have a larger project that needs more developers than we have on staff. Or maybe we need a part time or occasional resource for an ongoing task like DBA, report writing, etc.

- *Consultants* are the ones that bring in specific expertise on a product or service. Maybe we have a new software system we purchased and need consultants to help us implement. Maybe we want to bring a new portion of our ERP system online and need the expertise.

Contractors and consultants differ from products and services. We are hiring people that have skills for a particular reason and time frame. They will interact with our staff and perhaps others in our company. Here are some ideas to consider when creating and managing the pool of outside resources:

1. Curate the Vendor List

Create and manage a small pool of trusted companies to supply most consultants and contractors. Some vendors, especially for larger systems, offer consulting with their products. There will be large consulting firms that provide a wide range of skills for staff augmentation. There might be smaller companies that we build relationships with over time for a particular skill set.

Consider the list of vendors as strategic and tactical extensions of our teams. Consider the costs in the larger budgetary picture. Consider risk assessment when deciding to go outside for a skill or resource and for managing the use of a vendor.

2. Contractual Arrangements

We typically sign a Master Services Agreement that lays out the legal terms of all engagements and then specific addendum, typically called "Statement of Work" (SOW), cover the individual engagements. These make sense for specific projects or ongoing staff augmentation.

It can also be useful to create a SOW for ongoing support. Say we have just brought in some new technology and we want the expertise in house. We use the vendor for the initial implementation and our team learns alongside them. If we create a small time and material SOW with the vendor, our team will have a resource to draw on after the project. While vendors may be willing to just pick up the phone or answer an email, putting dollars to it will get a better response.

There is often that window where a team member will want some help to figure out something new or has a problem they haven't seen before. Having a few hours already arranged with the vendor makes it easier to reach out. I take care of the paperwork so that, in the moment of need, the team member doesn't have to worry about paperwork and can just get their help.

Since it is time and materials, it costs nothing if it doesn't get used. As long as we monitor it to make sure the time is being used wisely, it is usually money well spent.

A quick note about the agreements. Get good at reading and understanding Master Services Agreements. I have had more than a handful of vendors badly copy/paste from prior agreements or present an agreement that hasn't had a good reading in a long time. We will see enough of them in our career, so spend the time to get good at them.

3. T&M versus Fixed Bid

For Time and Materials (T&M) arrangements, the vendor charges us for the actual hours they spend on the project and the actual materials they purchase. For Fixed Bid, the vendor will charge us a fixed amount regardless of how much effort and materials they actually spend.

The benefit of T&M is that it matches the actual costs for the vendor. Good estimates from good vendors will often come in higher than what we will end up getting charged for. The vendor won't typically add padding for unforeseen circumstances unless it is a visible contingency that we can sign off on.

We get into trouble with T&M contracts when the project gets into trouble. We face tough decisions when the costs go over. Often we are too far down the path and it is hard to cut our losses and walk away with nothing.

Fixed bids are nice in that we know what we will pay. No guess work, no need to monitor the expenses or read through vendor time reports. The downside is that the vendor is likely covering themselves in case the project takes longer, so fixed bids are more expensive when the projects finish as expected.

Time & Materials projects are much better than fixed bid.

In my opinion, T&M is much better than fixed bid. I have worked with fixed-bid projects in my career, both as a Customer and as a vendor. Rarely does the bid come in perfect. If the project goes as expected, the extra padding that the vendor put in "just in case" costs the Customer more money. If the project goes much shorter or longer than expected, either the Customer or the vendor ends up unhappy.

The efficiency and effectiveness of the people on the project can make a big difference. Getting a person new to the vendor or someone who just doesn't understand the technology can be painful. Having an ongoing relationship with the vendor allows us to have those hard conversations before they become a bigger problem. Push back on the vendor and having them eat some hours often works in these situations.

4. Treat Vendors with Respect

I'm a believer in being nice to vendors. This isn't a universal view in this world where people view vendors as disposable resources to take advantage of. I have been on the vendor side of these arrangements. Finding good people, managing priorities, and navigating conflicting Customer needs is challenging. If we, as Customers, show we understand their challenges and will be flexible where we can to make the vendor's life a little easier, the vendor may return the favor. Put another way, by being one of their favorite Customers, we will get better treatment.

Someday, we will be in a bind, or will need to reject one of their people, or need to ask something hard from the company. These tough situations are easier if we have a good relationship with the vendor. Favorite Customers get treated better. I have gotten much better service, responses, and even financial benefits from being a good Customer that "gets it," i.e., understands the vendor's needs to be successful.

Vendors fire Customers all the time. They fire the ones that are high maintenance or the ones that are not profitable. They rarely come out and terminate an agreement, but they get slower or put their lower skilled people on our projects until we get annoyed and go away. If we treat vendors badly, they will be happy to see us go.

That doesn't mean that we don't stand up for our company. If we have a good relationship, then when we send that email that something is not acceptable or up to their normal standards, it gets attention and gets resolved.

When we need to deliver bad news to a vendor, we should do it ourselves. Our staff is working with the vendor daily, and it is better to keep them in the "good cop" role while we play the "bad cop."

Interns

If we are fortunate to live in an area with post-high school education, take advantage of it and get a paid intern or two. Having interns around has several benefits:

- Whether from a four-year college or a two-year technical school, interns are full of energy and excitement.
- They have grown up with technology in their pockets their entire life and are very comfortable with it.

- We can create a pipeline for future IT staff. Even if we don't have a position in the organization at the end of the internship, we have connected with someone that might help us in the years to come.
- By helping launch an intern into an IT career, we can affect the careers of more people than just our staff. Diversify the possible sources for interns.

In my experience, the full-year intern schedule works out the best. Starting at the end of the school year provides the entire summer of working full time, learning how the department works and how they fit in. When they go back to school in the fall, they can still be useful as part-time employees because of what they learned over the summer.

If we get them their senior year, take a bit of time and help them with their job hunting. Having seen hundreds of resumes and interviewed many candidates, we are in a unique position to help them.

When hiring interns, look for energy and drive. Getting good technical skills is important, but secondary. One risk with an intern is needing to push them to try new things, to go talk to people in the business, to write that email to someone they don't know. Finding an intern with energy and a willingness to try new things makes them more useful.

I have used interns in two roles: (1) Help Desk, and (2) Business Analyst. Two-year technical schools are great sources of Help Desk interns as the classes focus on technologies that apply to the Help Desk position.

What kinds of work do we have the interns do? There is the temptation to have them do all the boring grunt work. But this won't give them a satisfying experience and won't make the department better. Consider challenging them to reduce or eliminate the grunt work.

One year, for example, we had our Business Analyst intern work on a user account reconciliation project. We had a half dozen different systems with usernames and passwords. Some accounts were automatically added and removed when employees came and went, others were added manually and never cleaned up. Over the years, we hadn't been perfect in removing old accounts. We challenged the intern to create a tool that would take the user lists from all the systems and flag the ones that weren't active employees any more. We didn't provide a recipe for creating the spreadsheet, but we would answer questions and provide input if requested. The intern created a nice spreadsheet that took all the different account lists and compared it to the current employee roster, creating a list of accounts to clean up. It took a few weeks to create but eliminated a tedious manual process. A version of that tool is still in use today.

On the Help Desk side, we use interns to teach onboarding IT sessions, create documents, and solve help desk problems. We use them for computer setup and replacement activities.

Interns come with their own skills sets and interests. As with full-time employees, dig into that and build on their strengths. Find out what they want to do with their career and make sure they are showing progress in that direction. They are a great addition to the team.

Part 4

Technology

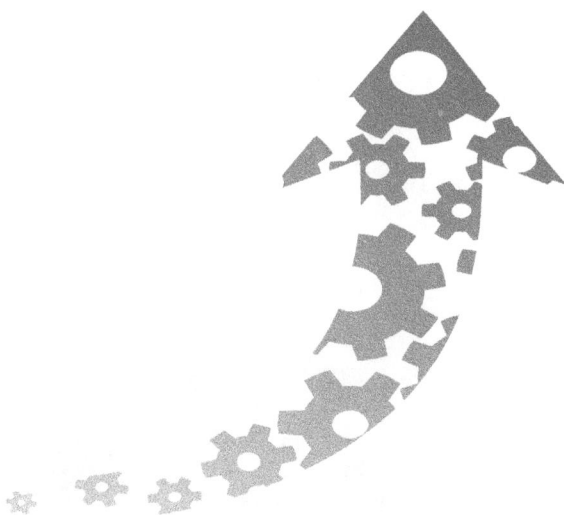

CHAPTER 19

TECHNOLOGY OVERVIEW

Technology is the last part of this book. While we need to have a strong understanding of technology, it is the area where we can rely on our staff more than Business and People.

To set your expectations, I will not be talking about any particular technology. This is not the book to learn about the digital transformation, cloud computing, or any of the other techno-buzzwords that most IT magazines and web sites write about. Any technology I might wish to talk about has been covered far better in a dozen places.

What I will talk about is how to think about the technology and how it affects the business and people. Technology is always changing, so we need to understand how to change technology to benefit the organization. If the people don't adopt the technology to improve their processes, it won't matter how slick or cool or transformative the technology is, it will fail.

I start with the chapter that asks *How Technical Do We Need To Be?* The chapter on our *Technology Portfolio* goes into the journey of our current state to where we want to be.

There are two major chapters on *Technology We Buy* and *Technology We Build*. The landscape for buying technology continues to get more complicated. While some organizations have tried to move away from building their own technology, this cuts out a major source of competitive innovation.

I'll wrap up this part of the book with chapters on *Shadow IT* and *When We Don't Need Technology*. But first, I want to talk about how technical we must be to be a good IT Leader.

CHAPTER 20

HOW TECHNICAL DO WE NEED TO BE?

Before we dive into how IT leaders think about technology, I want to answer a question that comes up from time to time. How technical do we need to be to lead an IT organization?

The simple and accurate answer is that our technical knowledge is merely one aspect of who we are, and a wide variety of technical expertise can be successful. But this answer isn't very helpful.

Just like Financial Directors need to know more about financial matters and HR Directors need to know more about people, IT Directors need to know more about technology and how to leverage it for the business. The key is knowing how to select and integrate technologies into the company so that the organization, and the people in it, can succeed.

> *The key is knowing how to select and integrate technologies into the company so that the organization, and the people in it, can succeed.*

'Integrate' is the big word here. As long as our company is using the technologies, we are integrating. Implementation, updates, expansion, and support are necessary and require people, time, money, and vendors. Our technical understanding of the products and services we use has an impact. But it isn't necessary to understand the details of technology to manage these tasks. It is necessary to understand the implications of the technology.

I think there is some benefit in coming up through the IT ranks. If we can get experience in both infrastructure and applications, we have a stronger foundation. When we get into management, we trust our team with the day-to-day technical work of the department.

We provide support for our teams, anticipate the problems they may have, and assign them tasks and projects. This puts them in the position to be successful. Our experience in the trenches doing the work gives us insights into what they face as they do their jobs.

Part of what I love about the job as an IT Director is that I can go from an annual business planning meeting to a conversation about a new technology to a chat about a particular networking problem to the test results from a new application to a hallway conversation about a business issue in another department. All in one day. I love the variety of topics and levels of detail I get to address in my job.

My experience with jobs inside and outside IT allows me to understand and contribute to conversations at all levels.

To be clear, my experience back in the day writing code using Fortran, Pascal, and Smalltalk doesn't really help me write C# or Dart code today. But the concepts I learned during those programming years still carry through. For example, user interactions, error logging, security, and data manipulation are in almost every programming language. If one of my team is developing in those languages, I can ask intelligent design and architecture questions during design and implementation phases.

As I was writing this, I wanted to check if this was still true. I watched a half hour of Dart videos because I had never laid eyes on the code itself. I wouldn't be able to write Dart code quickly, but there were a lot of familiar concepts in those videos. It feels good to not be a dinosaur yet.

Back to the question about how technical we need to be to lead an IT department. I've mentioned that if we can work our way up through the ranks, and give ourselves a variety of experiences, we will be in a better position to understand how technology fits into our organization.

It comes down to understanding the outline of technology, the impact of technology on the organization, and the ability to learn quickly.

But what if we don't have that experience? What if we get the opportunity to manage earlier in our career? What can we do then?

I think it comes down to understanding the *outline of technology*, the impact of technology on the organization, and the ability to learn quickly.

What do I mean by outline of technology? Think of the technology touch points in the organization. Think of technology's impact on business processes. Even better, think of the details behind the impact. Technology is only useful for what it can do for the organization in the big picture.

Let's look at several questions we need to understand, even if we don't understand the technology underneath the systems:

1. How do people think about and use the technology?

While user interfaces have transformed over the years, some things haven't changed. Users still need to understand where they enter inputs and see the outputs. The software needs to communicate errors effectively. It should be obvious what the user should do next. Users don't like change. These things are true for every user interface ever built.

Different people and different work styles call for different user interfaces. There will always be those that are more in tune with a particular user interface. There will always be those that will not like it or won't be able to get in sync with it. Neither opinion is right nor wrong, regardless of how we feel about it.

Introducing a new user interface always brings training issues, especially if it is a change from the way they used to do it. Brand new user interfaces are actually easier to implement than changing a heavily used one.

One challenge IT faces is that we typically like technology and some of our counterparts in the rest of the organization do not. It excites us to play with new tech! We love to learn new things! But we are not the rest of the rest of the business. Both at work and in their personal life, technology keeps changing and not always for the better. Think about smartphones, apps, watching TV, etc. These are constantly changing, and this can frustrate those that just want to make a phone call or watch a show.

As the 'constantly updating' concept moves from consumer technology to business technology, we face the same problems. Now, instead of changing via an upgrade every few years, we have applications and devices that are changing much more frequently, often outside our control. These changes can interrupt employee's work and increase the frustration with technology.

We need to understand the personal impact of technology on the individuals. Each person approaches technology in their own way. Some people are influencers or evangelizers.

We must have a good understanding of how our organization thinks about technology.

Questions:

- What is the user population for each piece of technology?
- What other places could we use a technology?
- How is this technology changing over time?
- How do people feel about the technology? It is always more nuanced than "some like it, some don't."
- How do the "influencers" feel about technology?

2. What business processes will the technology support?

Technology is used to make the business better. We build infrastructure like networks, servers, databases, Wi-Fi, and security to deliver applications the organization needs. Applications exist to enable business processes. Both have to be in place correctly and reliably for the organization to be successful.

Questions:

- How do employees, Customers, or suppliers interact to get work done? Understanding the touch points, the frictions, and exceptions is important. The system will affect the people and data in the business process.
- Do we understand all the people involved in each process?
- Do we know what software supports what processes? This can be tricky for common systems like email or file shares, but just as important to understand.
- What happens when there is a business process error that isn't a software error?
- How are exceptions handled?

3. Who will support it?

All technology needs some level of support. Usually this comes from IT, but sometimes departments handle it all themselves. Support refers to things like user account management, settings and parameters, security, backups, licensing, and configuration.

Questions:

- How much support do we need?
- Who is doing the support?
- How much time do we expect them to spend on support?
- What problems might pop up?
- Who is the expert when something goes wrong?

4. What other systems will it interface with?

The days of standalone systems have passed, although there are still some out there. Most systems in an organization interface with at least one other system.

This can be as simple as user accounts to make sure that the right employees have access or more complicated data that flows back and forth between systems.

Questions:

- What data moves between systems?
- When does the data move?
- What systems need to sync data?
- Who knows the technical details of the interface?
- How does our team know that the interface is working correctly?

5. What is the impact on our data?

Very few systems have no data of their own. Some will only consume data from other places but not add new — think of data warehouses and reporting systems. Most of the time, though, the data our organization uses comes from a variety of systems.

Questions:

- Where is the primary list of key data kept? For example, what system keeps the official list of employees and what systems keep copies and therefore need to stay in sync?
- Do the key fields for people, products, and departments all match?
- Are the business rules between the data elements the same between systems?
- Are the data repositories even the same type: relational, flat files, Bigtable, in-memory or something new to the organization?
- Is the data local or in the cloud?

CHAPTER 21

TECHNOLOGY PORTFOLIO

When I bought my first house, a wise person told me I should consider myself a temporary caretaker and keep the house well maintained while I lived there. If possible, I should try to sell the house in better shape than when I bought it. Whether I stayed in the house for two years or fifty years, new owners would eventually live there and the decisions and actions I took would directly affect their lives. Some parts, like painting and curtains, are easy to change. Some parts, like the plumbing, electrical, or the furnace would last for years and I needed to balance my financials with the long term when I made changes.

If the house is new, everything is shiny and fresh and there isn't much maintenance. I have never lived in a brand-new house, but I have lived in old houses. I lived in a house built in 1971, one built in 1888, and several in between. These houses had a motley collection of heating, electrical, plumbing and other systems. Prior owners had replaced or upgraded everything at least once.

When we step into the IT leadership role at a company, it is like buying the house. We are caretakers in a chain of caretakers. We have a responsibility to leave the organization in better shape than we found it, regardless of whether the technology portfolio is shiny and fresh or a haphazard mix of old and new.

Our technology portfolio is the collection of all purchased and built technologies that run the organization's information systems. Everything from the operating systems we use to the network infrastructure to that one weird app used to do some unique task. The technology portfolio also includes the consumer technology that sneaks in and around our company regardless of our attempts to manage it.

In this chapter, I will show how to think about your technology portfolio and aspects of managing it. Our portfolios are never static and always changing. Technology is always in motion.

The future portfolio is not something we can architect once and consider it finished. Let's look at a metaphor for this. Consider a sailing race. Imagine a large sailing ship with lots of sails and a sizable crew. We might think of a majestic sailing ship from days of old, or we might think of a sleek yacht. Doesn't matter. If it has sails, it is in the race.

We have a responsibility to leave the organization in better shape than we found it, regardless of whether the technology portfolio is shiny and fresh or a haphazard mix of old and new.

This race isn't for a certain distance or certain time. This is a permanent race. It never stops and has been going on for years.

Over time, everything changes. Crew members come and go. Some have been sailing for years, some are new to the game. New competitors join and old competitors drop out. The rules constantly change. There is no finish line, but there are rewards for being the fastest. New technologies to enable greater speeds are coming out regularly.

But the race never stops. There are no breaks from the race, so we can't stop to swap out major components like the hull or sails. We need to figure out how to change them while continuing to race.

And, of course, at some point, some bright person comes up with the idea to add an engine to the ship and completely change the race. New competitors enter that have only engines and no sails. The race has dramatically changed, and we must change to stay competitive — while we are still racing.

We are in charge of the physical ship. Others are in charge of the crew, giving orders, figuring out destinations, etc.

In our world: We are in charge of the technical portfolio. Others are in charge of the people, processes, finances, markets, selling, etc. The race never takes a break, and we need to maintain (and sometimes replace) every part of the technology portfolio over time.

Whew! Sounds daunting, doesn't it?

IT leaders have been doing this for decades and will continue to do so as far into the future as we can see. Some are more successful than others. Let's look at a framework for how we can approach this impossible problem.

1. What is our current portfolio?

The first step is to know what we have. We must have an accurate inventory of the technologies used in our organization. It doesn't need to be a single list that contains everything. Such a list becomes too cumbersome to work with. Let's start at a higher level and see the major groupings and a few examples:

- Infrastructure: networks, storage, servers, virtual and cloud environments, backup, load balancers.
- End user devices: desktops, laptops, tablets, smartphones.
- Security: malware tools, penetration testing tools and services, authentication, password management, VPNs, badges.
- Applications: large systems like an ERP, word processing, spreadsheets, email, collaboration, analysis tools, special purpose applications.
- Technology Management Tools: systems monitoring, log file analysis, error reporting, license management.

- Development tools: programming languages, data visualization tools, end user database access products.

It does not take very long in a company's growth for this list to grow to many dozens or hundreds of products. IT alone may use dozens of applications and utilities itself. It is very hard to maintain a completely accurate portfolio list.

My preference is to have several lists. Infrastructure components go into a network diagram. A 'fleet management' tool keeps an automatically updated inventory of end user devices and installed software. Separate lists for applications and services can be helpful for seeing the big picture. Architecture documents for larger systems capture interfaces between systems. A security model captures the tools and services used to protect the organization.

Having such lists makes it easier for different parts of the IT organization to ensure their information is accurate. The troublesome part comes in understanding the different lists and how they relate. That often falls on our shoulders as there are few in our departments that understand the big picture.

Another point to consider is who can bring new technology into the company. Is it only IT or can other groups do so? The benefits of distributed acquisition are that newer technology may be brought in faster and directly in the parts of the organization that will use it.

I am strongly in the IT-only camp for bringing in new technology. The resulting consistency of the portfolio is the clearest benefit.

If IT is the only group bringing in new technology, we provide centralized control. This has the benefit of more effective acquisition and better alignment across the company, better utilization of company resources, and better support. Culture drives this topic far more than the technology. Each organization will have a different answer.

I am strongly in the IT-only camp for bringing in new technology. The resulting consistency of the portfolio is the clearest benefit.

2. What is our future portfolio?

So now we know what we have in our portfolio today. How do we determine what our future portfolio should look like? We have already established that a single, static view of the future portfolio is short-sighted. While there are many reasons for choosing different technology directions, it is important to stay on top of three major areas.

In the Business part of this book, I presented the first area already: Know the business. Understand the trends and transitions the business is facing. This should be the first and loudest input into our thinking.

Next are the big technology trends going on in the world. These trends shape the products we can buy. Our opinion of them will have little effect. These trends will continue. Examples include:

- Physical to virtual to cloud computing
- Desktop to laptop to tablet to smartphone
- Centralized to distributed and back again

Finally, vendor changes outside our control may force us to react. These issues never come up at a convenient time. Ideally, we decide it is the best thing to do for the business and then it becomes a required change. However, it rarely works like that. Sometimes we have no choice, and it adds no value to the business. Forced upgrades are a good example.

Sometimes you get a chain of dependencies that just make you shake your head. System A doesn't support a certain version of an operating system and we can't upgrade system B until we upgrade system A. At one company, I had a chain that prevented us from upgrading a certain security module until we replaced $10,000 worth of phones. There was an Active Directory schema update and two software upgrades in the chain.

I would like to tell you that with proper planning, this will never happen to us. But that would not be the truth. We can do our best to stay ahead of it, to keep all the infrastructure at the latest and greatest versions, but it will not be sufficient. It happens to all of us at some point.

Those three things — know the business, know the trends, and know the vendors — will help us make better decisions on our future technology portfolio.

It is useful if we document this future state, but that is even harder than documenting current state. I recommend applying risk management to this situation. Focus on documenting the higher risk areas, so we have a clear roadmap for technology critical to our organization.

But more important than just documenting the future, we need to understand and act on it. I have seen current and future state portfolios assembled but not understood by the leaders. It was a technical exercise that got put on a shelf and not used.

With a good understanding of the future portfolio, we have a better foundation for the many decisions we need to make on the journey. The dynamic nature of technology means that our future portfolio will always be changing.

3. The journey to the future portfolio

Keeping our changing destination in mind, let's look at how we plan our journey. The journey will have upgrades, new purchases, and other projects to move us towards a better portfolio.

The change in technology products is fast, and the line between business and consumer technology is rapidly blurring. Products that we have been using in our business for over two years have a least one upgrade from the vendor and probably some new competing products. There are likely one or two products that provide a fresh way to approach that technology niche.

Obviously we will not replace everything every two years. Even though we can make an argument for upgrading or replacing almost everything in our technology portfolio, rarely is there a good business case for doing so.

But we need to keep certain things current. We know the older technology that needs replacing. We know the products we have that no longer have a viable vendor or vendor strategy. We know there are new products out there that will have a large impact on our organizations.

And there will always be new shiny products to look at. The employees in our companies, or our bosses, are always glad to point them out.

There will always be pressure, sometimes from our own team, to bring in the latest technology.

While there are several considerations for deciding to bring in a new product or technology, there is one at the top of the list.

What business need does the technology meet now and in the future?

The IT department exists to make the organization successful. Therefore, we must make all technology decisions with that in mind. But we can interpret the phrase "make the organization successful" in several ways. Creating the unique interpretation for our organization is one of the most important technology decisions we can make.

How do we prioritize everything to make effective progress? How do we lay out the journey to the future portfolio?

First, we start with the projects that we must get done, usually for external reasons. Let's call these the 'Must-Do' projects.

Second, we make sure that our foundation is strong. Networks, security, databases, and other components sit under all the applications. They must be solid.

Next, we work on long-term projects. This includes replacing major systems, introducing workflow tools, and other larger pieces. We can do only one or two of these a year because of the magnitude of change management and the resource demands.

urgent important matrix

Finally, there are the smaller projects that build on the foundation and major systems.

Eisenhower's Urgent/Important matrix helps us here. If you are not familiar with this way to think about tasks and projects, it is worth your time to look at the pros and cons of it.

	Urgent	Less Urgent
Important	Work On Now	Plan now to avoid it becoming urgent
Less Important	Outsource?	Delay

The two-by-two matrix captures the urgency and importance of a situation. Our 'Must-Do' projects fall into the "Important & Urgent" box. Foundation and Long-Term projects fall into the "Important & Not Urgent" box.

'Must-Do' projects disrupt our portfolio journey. We can avoid most of them by planning on projects before they become urgent, but, since they don't add value to the company, it is easy for us to delay them until they become urgent. Let's look at a few reasons they pop up:

- The vendor discontinues the product and drops support. The product relies on a cloud technology that is getting turned off on a certain date. Read up on the history of Flash for an example of this.

- The vendor hasn't added support for a new version of the operating system, forcing us to stay at the old version. This prevents us from upgrading a different application that doesn't support the old version anymore.

- An internally developed application, written in an obsolete programming language by a person who no longer works for the company, requires a purchased product that is no longer available and won't install on the current operating system.

- A regulation in one of our markets changes to require significant security enhancements. For example, in the last few years, the defense industry has added significant cyber-security requirements.

- A malware attack requires that we update to a new operating security level, which breaks an application. We must choose between using the application or closing an attack vector.

- A vendor does a major rewrite and forces all existing Customers to upgrade. The new version is different enough that business processes need to change in a way that adds no value.

- An ERP upgrade, needed for additional features, drops support for the old user interface that our company has been using comfortably for years.

The list goes on and on. We won't always be able to avoid these types of situations, so we must keep track of what is going on with vendors of our important systems.

The Foundations and Long-Term projects are harder to sell because the bulk of the benefits lie in the future. For example, the day after we finish a network switch replacement project, there won't be much benefit to the company. That comes later, when we can take advantage of the higher speeds or make changes faster and better. Another example is upgrading a major system. We probably won't be able to take advantage of additional features until we implement additional projects to update business processes.

Short-term projects, the last one on our list, are typically easier to sell as they have more tangible benefits to the company. But we can't work on these until the Foundation and Long-Term projects are complete.

We need to tell the story of the larger journey to leadership. This story must draw a straight line from the Foundations and Long-Term projects to specific benefits for the company.

Consider starting with the benefits and working backwards to show the structure. Explain how we will get there. If leadership understands the journey, and the reasoning behind it, they won't stop believing in it.

> *If leadership understands the journey, and the reasoning behind it, they won't stop believing in it.*

CHAPTER 22

TECHNOLOGY WE BUY

The next two chapters will cover how to bring technology into our organizations. This chapter is on the technology we buy and the next will be on the technology we build, primarily software. I won't be covering specific technologies; I will cover the framework for making selection and implementation decisions about any technology.

Bringing a new technology into our business means selecting and implementing a specific product from a specific vendor. This is never as smooth as we hope. *Technologies* are awesome and perfect with lots of potential and possibilities. *Specific products* have problems and never work exactly as we want them to. *Vendors* want to be profitable and are never doing what we think they should be.

Selecting and implementing specific products from vendors is something that we need to do well. In this chapter, I will cover some issues we need to address as we go through the process.

Most projects spend large amounts of time on the selection. They will have a large cross-functional group that creates a massive list of requirements and painstakingly goes through the vendors, probably creating some kind of scoring system to rank them. Demos, sand-box trials, and lots of meetings will go into selecting a new product.

Then they hand it off to IT and go back to their jobs. It's just implementation, right? Just get it up and running and let everyone use it. How hard can it be?

Generally, I am a cheerful person. I understand normal business pressures and the unfair view of IT that sometimes results. But this situation is one that grinds my gears. They have it backwards.

I believe the following is true: A great system, implemented badly, will likely fail. A mediocre system, implemented beautifully, will likely succeed.

Selecting Technology

In making portfolio decisions, we looked at the benefits and costs of bringing in a new technology. Now let's look at selecting a vendor.

Searches and selections can be a lot of work. And it is important to get them right. So what can we do to make vendor searches more effective?

We know about the long list/short list concept where we create our long list of products and narrow it down to the short list. Colleagues, peers, articles, web searches, and the inevitable ads that start popping up once we start internet searching can all inform our long list. We set the selection criteria and cost parameters and narrow it down to the short list. Then we do demonstrations, dog & pony vendor presentations, reference checks, etc. to further weed out the ones that don't work.

> *A great system, implemented badly, will likely fail. A mediocre system, implemented beautifully, will likely succeed.*

Once we have the short list, I strongly suggest that the goal at this point is not to pick the winner. The goal should be to remove the ones that won't work. This leaves a list of products that will work. This is a better goal than picking a winner, as we will see when we talk about implementation. If there is only one that will work, great, our decision is easy. Chances are, however, there will be several that will work in our organization.

But first, I want to present some concepts to think about as we move from our long list to our short list. These are, of course, besides our functional requirements and cost constraints.

1. How critical is the choice of product to the business?

If we get it wrong, what is the risk to the company? The more critical the product, the more we need to invest in the selection process. An ERP system or central billing system are good examples of a critical piece of software that will have a major impact on our company. We need to spend the time to get the selection right. At the other end of the extreme, maybe we need something like electronic MSDS sheets or access to online standards. Obviously, the selection process for smaller products should be shorter than the one for our central system. Remember the concept of opportunity cost. The time we spend on the selection process is time that we don't spend on anything else.

This can be hard. The desire to pick the absolute best product can be strong. We want to put in all the time and work to get it right. But we don't need to, and sometimes we shouldn't. We should put in the time to meet our definition of success and not a minute longer.

Questions:

- How many parts of the business will this product touch?
- If the system has a major problem, what will be the impact on the organization?
- How long do we expect to have this product?
- How hard will it be to switch to another product down the road?

2. What system interfaces will we need?

Very few systems exist in isolation. We should have some expectations on what systems we will need to connect and how those connections will work. Unfortunately, this is an area where vendors are not especially helpful. Vendors will tell us they can interface to anything. Vendors will tell us the interfaces will work the way we want. They will throw terms like "flexible" and "open" at us like treats to a dog being trained.

There is one thing, though, that we can count on. The philosophy of the interface, the basic way it is organized and how it works, will not be what we want to interface with our other systems. Especially if they use something modern like web services. The vendor will claim the interface can do anything we want. But until we write some prototype code that proves otherwise, we must assume it will not match what we need.

The vendor will claim the interface can do anything we want. But until we write some prototype code that proves otherwise, we must assume it will not match what we need.

We likely won't get a chance to test all interfaces during the selection process to prove any of this. Very few vendors let us sandbox test their interfaces or release the documentation for our review without buying. Our best bet is to find references that have used the interface and have a deeper discussion or, even better, a show and tell.

Questions:

- What methods are available for interfacing the product to our other systems?
- How good is the documentation for these interfaces?
- What kinds of problems do other companies run into when interfacing to existing systems?
- What do other companies' interface implementations look like? Are they more or less complicated than our plans?

3. How common is the product or technology?

Are we looking for networking systems, security software, or an ERP system? These markets have lots of players. If most IT departments are implementing it, then there likely are a few major players that need to be on our long list. But if everyone is buying something in this product category, there will also likely be some startups trying to disrupt the marketplace. If we put a few of the startups on the list, we might see a novel way of thinking about an old problem.

Questions:

- Who are the market leaders?
- Who are the market disrupters?
- How much variety is there between products?
- How does each vendor win against the others?
- Which vendors are growing? Why?

4. How mature are the products in this technological space?

In a new market, there is typically a company that starts it out and several other smaller companies that jump in quickly. As the market matures and vendors see that it is a legitimate long-term market, others, including the big vendors, will join in. As the market matures, there will be a few vendors that have the bulk of the market share.

Email and word processing software have been around a long time, and there really haven't been significant changes. There are only a few vendors to choose from. On the other hand, security software is constantly changing and startups with novel ways of approaching security are hitting the market regularly. By understanding how mature a product space is, we can set expectations for how much effort we put into creating our long list.

If it is a relatively new product space, it may not be clear who the market leaders are. There might not be common features. For example, Augmented and Virtual Reality products are new, different, and risky at the time I am writing this. The marketplace will look very different a year from now.

There will always be big players in the technology space. They are more cautious about where they invest their development dollars. If we look at a new product space and start seeing the large companies getting into the market through investment or acquisition, the market is moving into the mature state.

Questions:

- How long has each product been on the market?
- Was the product developed internally or was it acquired?
- How has the competitive landscape changed over the last few years?
- If you look at reviews from three years ago, were the same vendors winning?

5. What is the technology trajectory?

Products and technologies have a current state, but are never static. They also never exist in a vacuum. Even products that seem revolutionary fit into an overall technical evolution that we can see. I'm not talking about the ability to predict what products will come out — that would be outstanding and lucrative! I'm talking about larger trends that are influencing a particular market space.

If we look at the market that a technology exists in, we will see various products at different stages in their life cycle. Even in niches where a company claims that their product is brand new to the world, we can usually find other products that can give a sense of the trend. Is this a mature market with lots of well-developed products that compete by adding features? Is it a new market where products have very different design philosophies? Is the market big enough that the big companies have gotten into the game? Or is the market small and there will never be lots of investment in the products? Are the products being built by small teams or by larger organizations that have deep pockets?

Products and technologies have a current state, but are never static.

These kinds of questions can give us a sense of how long this product will be around. Maybe it will give us a sense that it is rapidly changing and we might not want to make a multi-year commitment.

Security software is an example of fast-changing technology. Malware continues to evolve quickly, and the tools to fight it must evolve to keep up. There are lots of companies in this space and they are putting a lot of money into bringing out new or upgraded products regularly. When we sign up for a security product, we should assume that in a couple of years we will need to update to a different product. It may even be from the same vendor if we are lucky.

On the other hand, implementing our central system or large data warehouse product is a longer-term investment. The product spaces aren't as dynamic as security systems, and our internal investment is bigger. The time and skills our company needs to develop are much more significant, so the cost of changing is much higher.

Questions:

- Do the vendors' product roadmaps match the company's long-term needs?
- What does each vendor think is going to happen in the product space?
- How has the competition changed over the last year?
- When was the last major refresh of each product? Too long and they aren't staying current. Too recent and there may be problems still shaking out.

6. How does the vendor make their money?

When choosing a significant technology, knowing how each vendor makes money is important. Here are some ways vendors make their profits:

- One-time purchase price
- Initial price plus annual maintenance
- Implementation fees

- Regular payments (a.k.a. subscriptions)
- Consulting
- Selling our information

Most companies want to get us on the regular payment schedules. Signing up for these subscriptions can give us lower initial payments, but those payments never end. This makes the financial analysis of the purchase more difficult than a normal purchase. When the cost in all future years is the same as year one, what does the return on investment look like? If our organization grows or shrinks, how does that impact our return on investment?

The more cloud-based systems we use, the more of an ongoing monthly expense we will have. These vendors are hosting our data and their software in the cloud and therefore have regular expenses. They use this as a reason to charge us each month. It also gives them a predictable income stream, allowing them to make better investments.

Maybe the vendor makes more money from their consulting practice than the software they sell? Maybe they will give away their services because they make their money from advertising or selling our information.

By knowing how a vendor makes money, we will understand where our levers are in negotiating. They won't typically be willing to give on their primary profitability source, but everything else may be on the table.

Questions:
- How does each vendor make their money?
- Which part of the quotes have the most room to negotiate?
- It may be hard to get satisfactory answers to the above questions. So we have to be more indirect. Where are their sales? Are they phasing any pricing in or out? What is the biggest part of their sales push?

7. Risk Tolerance

The way our organization views technology risk is part of its personality. Is it a company that likes shiny new toys and has the money and people to invest? Or is it a company that has such low margins that we can't afford too much in the way of technology? Our company's tolerance for risk will affect how we select vendors. There are a couple of places we can end up on the scale of risk tolerance. Keep in mind that risk tolerance may be different even within our organization, so it can vary from one selection to another if it involves different departments.

Using a knife analogy, our companies can be in different places. Let's take a look at the different risk profiles. I'm sure you will quickly identify your company.

When our company is on the bleeding edge, we want to try out the latest products. We are willing to be a beta tester for releases, even our ERP. We may have the latest phones and the latest mobile apps. We are comfortable trying out first-in-a-niche products. This all requires a technical team that can learn new technology and, more importantly, be able to support it in the business. We negotiate discounts to help a startup get established in the market.

If we are on the leading edge, we prefer to see a year or two on a product to know that the product is solid. We don't beta test the next version of the ERP, but we start our upgrade as soon as the vendor releases it to everyone. We are looking for places to improve our company and will try new systems, just not too new.

Companies with mainstream risk tolerance go for established products with good track records. We actively work to reduce the risk of new products by research. We rarely add startups to our long list, and they never make the short list.

Finally, if we are in a lagging company, we watch for technology that is being left behind, often because we can get it cheaper. The products are well known in the industry and there are many people that know how to use it. We run into the problem of vendors dropping support or disappearing altogether. We hate startups and are familiar with the used equipment market.

Questions:

- When we suggest a new system, what kinds of pushback do we get?
- Do we get suggestions from the rest of the organization about a cool new technology we should try?
- Are the leaders of the company pushing technology?
- Is there much Shadow IT going on?

8. How big is the vendor's development team?

We can learn a lot about how the vendor thinks by the size of the development team. They don't always provide that information, or they give us a number that handles all their products. So we have to dig sometimes. I've had some luck getting a salesperson to give me an order of magnitude: single digits? dozens? hundreds? Looking on LinkedIn to see how many job openings they have may provide a clue.

The larger the development team, the more the vendor thinks it will need new features and, therefore, the more we can expect in the future. The smaller the team, the more likely the vendor is winding down development because they think they can't compete in the market or the market is changing.

There is a scenario to watch out for, especially in software products. If a product has a long lifetime, each vendor will decide at some point they need to reimplement their product. The technology and design decisions they made at the beginning are no longer sufficient to keep them competitive. They will use words like "re-architecting," "redesign," and "next generation." They will shift most of their development resources to the new version. When we see this shift, we need to plan for an upgrade or a replacement system. Even if the older version seems better at the moment, it is functionally dead as a product (regardless of what the vendor says).

In the situations where we already have the old product and have decided that the redesign is the right move, beware that it won't be all sunshine and roses. It will be missing features we use or have incomplete features that will frustrate our users. Just remember that all the vendor's development resources are on the new version and they probably only have a skeleton crew on our version. Keep the pressure on them to resolve issues.

So, back to the development team size. Startups are hard to judge because the development team is small. But if it is a brand-new product niche, and it meets our needs, that vendor may be the right choice. I view startups, regardless of how great their product is, as temporary, and make a note to replace it in several years. Most startups fail or get swallowed up by the big vendors. Sometimes we can get lucky and a new startup succeeds and sticks around for a while. When this happens, we get bonus time on our decision.

Questions:

- How big is the development team working on the product?
- Is the product development team growing or shrinking?
- Is the inevitable redesign in the recent past or in the future?

9. Are there resources outside the vendor that can provide help and/or support?

Sometimes, we will want outside help to implement a system, especially larger ones. What kind of help is available? Does the vendor have a professional services team? Are there third parties that can provide expertise? Some larger consulting companies offer consulting practices for a wide variety of products. Having competition is always good.

Once, I had a label software product that needed upgrading. We knew we didn't need the expertise in house to do a major upgrade. We only needed expertise in-house on how to run it, create and manage labels, and troubleshoot. Because of other priorities, we had gotten behind by a few versions and the upgrade was more complicated. So when it came time to upgrade, we contacted the vendor to handle it.

There was no third-party consulting available, and the vendor's professional services team was booked up. With no competition, they were expensive. And there was not much we could do about it. We had to bite the bullet and move forward with them.

So when looking at selecting a product and vendor, look at what third-party consulting is available. The more the better.

Questions:

- Are there any third-party support organizations?
- If we don't have resources to help us in a timely fashion, what are our other options?
- Do the major integration companies offer support?

10. Can we experiment with a technology without a commitment?

Look for opportunities that allow our organization to play with new technology before making any kind of financial commitment. This is especially important in new-to-the-world technology.

At the time of writing this book, Augmented Reality (AR) was just moving out of the gaming industry and into manufacturing. There were some groundbreaking products, but only a few companies were doing anything with it. When the pandemic hit, large parts of the engineering and support organizations needed to work from home. This made support on the production floor much more difficult.

One of our software vendors came out with a workflow that brought AR to remote support. They had made a limited functionality workflow useful in a remote support situation. In a good-for-everyone move, they made it free to their Customers for a short period. Because we had a good relationship with this vendor, they came to us as they were developing it. The result was that we got to play, for the first time, with AR to see how it worked for us.

We didn't move forward with the product, but we got some valuable experience with the technology and this informed our future decisions.

These opportunities don't come along often, but having a good relationship with our vendor increases the possibilities.

Questions:

- Is there a way that we can demo the product ourselves?
- Can we set up our environment in the product to make sure it works for us?

11. How much experience does the vendor have with our kind of company?

It is important to get a sense of what type of companies a vendor can handle. Regardless of what business we are in, the vendors work with other companies that are not like us. We need to understand how well the vendor knows companies like ours.

Questions:

- How many companies like ours (size, business type) have successfully implemented your product?
- Can you provide us with a list of other Customers similar to us?
- Can you set up a meeting with another company that is very similar to ours so we can see how they have implemented your product?

12. What is the true cost to our organization?

The last item on our list is cost. Every piece of technology we bring into our company has both tangible, cash-out-the-door costs and intangible costs of people's time and impact on other technologies. It is the intangible costs that can cause the most problems for us.

Remember the car commercials that talked about "lower cost of ownership" as a selling point, such as better gas mileage and

Every piece of technology we bring into our company has intangible costs of people's time and impact on other technologies. It is the intangible costs that can cause the most problems for us.

cheaper repairs? Selecting a car with better gas mileage or cheaper repairs might have a lower cost of ownership, depending on the initial price. If we looked at every dollar we were going to put into the vehicle over the time we owned it, we would have the cost of ownership. How would that impact our buying decision? Sometimes, our financial situation doesn't allow us to choose the option with the overall lower cost of ownership. But we are aware of it.

IT systems are no different. There are ongoing costs we must pay for any implementation. Sometimes the costs are concrete, cash-out-the-door costs like software maintenance. Sometimes, they are harder to pin down, like code that is less flexible to future changes or limitations to future process changes.

Let's look at some technology costs that we need to understand:

1. Initial purchase price. This one is easy. It's just the purchase price and the implementation price, right? Not so much anymore. Cloud systems bring a subscription model with ongoing costs that never stop. How much are we going to spend for the system over the years? How do we compare that against an on-premise system? The vendors all really want a subscription model. Is that really in our best interest?

Different license models are showing up in the marketplace. Options now include per user, per transaction, per gigabyte stored, per megabyte transferred, and so forth. It can be difficult when comparing vendors with differing models, as we have to do the translation and comparison ourselves.

These different models also bring *time* into the equation. It is possible to get started at a low cost and then increase as we roll a system out to the company. But the vendors are speaking out of both sides of their mouth. They brag about the low cost of entry, but they also want you to commit to a larger number over a longer period of time.

There is a tension between organizations wanting to buy licenses as they grow and these vendors wanting to sell the total licenses at the beginning. For example, fifty people may eventually use a new software application, but we are starting off with a pilot program with five people. The vendor will push for the commitment of fifty, offering discounts as incentives. The people in our organizations who think this software is a great idea will also want to just get the fifty at the start. We should have a good understanding of our organization to know how likely it will be that we will get to fifty users. Sometimes projects don't make it past the pilot stage, and we will waste those extra licenses.

2. Maintenance. Traditional technology purchasing has an annual maintenance fee. Software can be 18%-22% of the purchase price, billed annually. Hardware usually needs maintenance costs for the inevitable breakdowns. These are like the extended warranty you can buy for your TV, but you are risking your business and not just your favorite show.

Vendors have used these maintenance costs to pay for new product development for years.

3. Cost of upgrade. If we have purchased a good system from a good vendor, there will be new products and versions. How expensive is it to move to the new version? Hardware is often a replacement cost item. Software will be maintenance or subscription, but sometimes for small applications our only choice is to buy each new version at full cost. The larger the system, the more expensive it will be to upgrade.

4. Cost of Change. Over the life of the product, we will probably need to change configuration or settings. Do we build the expertise in our team or do we use outside expertise? How much testing do we need and who will do it? Will we need to build the expertise internally (training costs and time) or bring in outside help (money out the door)?

The initial use of the system will change over time as the business changes. Is the effort for us to change the system easy or hard? The cost of "the system doesn't let us do that" is hard to quantify, but it is real.

5. Cost of Administration. How big is the administrative task? Does the system sit quietly and behave and require little of our team's time, like a quiet koala sitting in a tree? Or is it more like a raccoon constantly causing problems? Each system we have puts an administrative load on our organization. These add up.

6. Third Party Costs. Do we need to use an outside company to help maintain the system? For example, for a complex uninterrupted power supplies, we likely don't have someone on staff that can repair or expand the system and will use the vendor. Or it may not be worth having a full-time database analyst (DBA) on staff, so we setup a DBA service that we can use as needed.

7. Debug-ability. What tools are available in the system to help solve the inevitable problems? How good are the log files? Can we detect problems before the users do? Some systems are easier to troubleshoot than others. One anti-virus software my team installed was a pain. There were a handful of computers that wouldn't install and configure the software correctly, and there were not good troubleshooting tools available. A few years later, we switched to another product. It installed with fewer problems, and there was a console with excellent diagnostics.

8. No Value Maintenance. If the system runs for several years, are there things we need to do that add no value? The classic case for this one is growing log files. Unless the vendor or our team puts in automated cleanup, we will need to implement log file monitoring or we will fill up a disk. This can also be a small money drain if it is in the cloud with infinite storage available.

Is there a report writing system? Then there probably are unused reports we need to clean up. We need to do it, but it adds no value to the business.

9. Scalability. Will the system grow with our company? If the company is growing slowly, there is little risk. But if we are experiencing significant growth, there can be some unpleasant surprises. Per-user software license costs can go down for multi-user systems as the numbers get bigger. However, hardware systems or systems that depend on embedded databases or other functionality may reach thresholds that require additional investments. If your company is growing quickly, make sure to ask these questions.

After the Selection

So far in this chapter, we have covered the factors we need to consider when selecting a product and vendor. Selecting a product and vendor is a risk management process. We need to decide when we don't have 100%

of the needed information, in a space where technology, products, and vendors are constantly changing, and we need to do it in a timely manner.

Mitigating some risk by the above concepts will help reduce the risk of a poor selection.

However, even making an excellent selection is only part of the solution. We need to implement it correctly as well.

Implementing Technology

When we are doing our search, the goal is to select the one product that is best for our company. So we are comparing the products against each other. Excellent, that is important. But there is another question that is equally important: can we be successful with this product? This is a yes/no question that we ask of all products on our short list. The answer for each product is independent of the other products.

Asking this question after we have created our short list has the potential to save time and effort on the selection. To understand this, let's look at two scenarios. Well, one scenario collapses quickly into the other, so there is only one scenario that matters.

We have our short list. The team spends an appropriate amount of time asking "Will this product work for us?" for each one. It should be obvious that the answer for each one on our shortlist should be YES. If any are NO, then they come off the shortlist. So now we are down to the only scenario that matters: a few products we know will each work for the business.

Great! Now what?

Well, now is where I toss a wildcard into the mix. Most times, when we get down to the final 2-3 products, knowing they all can do the job, it makes more sense to put extra time into implementation planning and less time into the final selection. I'm not saying that we should select the winner via the flip of a coin or a roll of the dice. Cost and functionality still matter and may point to a clear winner. I am, however, saying that we should make that decision mostly through the lens of implementation.

Why focus so much on implementation? Because *how* we implement is as important, if not more important, than the product we select. Remember, we already believe we can be successful with each product on our short list.

So rather than set up even more demos and feature shootouts, start putting together the implementation plan and see how the products fit in.

As I said at the beginning of this chapter: A great system, implemented badly, will likely fail. A mediocre system, implemented beautifully, will likely succeed.

Let's look at what goes into a good implementation project and I think it will become clear:

1. Define Success

First, we should have done this step before we started the selection process. But if we didn't, now is the time to do it.

How will we know that the project is successful? This is never just "the system is live." Did we completely update to the new business processes and are they being used successfully? Is the old system turned off? Is all documentation updated? Is everyone trained? Is all the data cleaned up?

Make sure everyone agrees on the definition of success. Make a list of what deliverables need to be complete to consider the project complete. There will be must-haves and nice-to-haves that we need to keep separate and clear to all. Use this as a guide: if we would slip the go live date because an item isn't complete, then it is a must-have. If we would keep the go live date and figure it out afterwards, it is a nice-to-have.

Be sure to talk ahead of time about the inevitable scope creep requests. They will happen and they aren't all bad. Put a decision process in place to deal with them.

Should-haves, scope creep items, and go live issues will blur the line for when the project ends. We can move some items to the ongoing support and enhancements list. If we don't have a good handle on this, the project will continue forever.

2. Stakeholders

Stakeholders are those in the organization that the new system will affect. It is important to have stakeholder involvement in the project.

But it is not important to have 100% of all stakeholders involved in all the decision making, planning, and execution. There will be some at the fringes that have more important things to do than a tiny piece of the project.

So how do we decide who to involve? There will be those that feel they need to be involved in every project, even if it won't affect them much. There will be those that should be involved but won't want to commit the time. For larger projects, getting this right becomes complicated.

Let's look at three distinct groups of stakeholders and how we might involve them:

- People using the process. We must represent the people that execute the primary processes that are changing. Depending on who we can draw from, we might have one person or we might need several people to make sure we have good risk assessment, decision making, and testing.

- People using the affected secondary processes. If there are business processes upstream or downstream of the ones changing, having them involved at strategic points in the project is important. They can be useful in setting requirements and verifying interfaces. We need not involve them in the internal process decisions of the primary group.

- Management. Management brings the organization's concerns to the table. Understanding what is important in the bigger picture ensures the project doesn't go off into the weeds. We can use a steering team to have management influence on the project. Management can also be useful as leaders on the implementation team to drive agreement from others.

We will involve these three groups in various ways at various times in the project. Selecting the right people for the teams revolves around risk tolerance, technical comfort, attitude towards change, thought leadership on their teams, and investment in the project's success.

The scale and scope of the project will influence the size and complexity of the stakeholders' involvement. For example, replacing network switches with a new architecture will technically affect everyone, but since that impact should be invisible, our stakeholder pool is perhaps just those from IT.

One last thing, go back and read the chapter on the Square Root of Change (chapter 2). Those that are struggling with the change can be useful in risk reduction.

3. Training

Any technology we bring into our organization will require that someone learn something. We need to identify the *someone* and scope the *something*.

In most cases, the *someone* will be both IT and the business. If the technology is visible to end users, there will be some end user training involved. If we change a major business process, the training will need to be significant.

IT will need to learn how to administer the system. Help Desk will need to learn how to resolve the issues that pop up. The Applications team will need to learn what the technology is capable of to apply it to the business processes correctly.

Training needs to cover the concepts and mechanics of using the product. How will we drive that knowledge into the organization? We have a wide range of learning styles and technical comfort levels in the company. How will we reach all of them?

We can't leave our training plan until the end of the project. The more our end users understand the technology, the more they can teach others. Training users early starts that process.

It is best if the individual departments have experts on how they use the technology in their area. If IT remains the experts, our support efforts will be high.

Plan ahead, make sure people know what we expect them to learn.

4. Data

If our networks are the train tracks, then our data are the trains running on those tracks. Our systems are passing data back and forth, updating, replicating, or syncing constantly. There will be a data component of almost every technology we implement.

At the start of implementation planning, we should know what data will need to be moving around. Perhaps we will only need to keep the user accounts in sync with our central identification system. Perhaps there will be a sizable amount of data flowing into and out of the central system.

A standard data flow diagram will show the systems and the data that needs to flow between them. That tells us the interfaces we need in the final configuration.

But that only shows part of the story. Data will transform as it moves around. We will need to import old data. We won't be able to migrate some old data, and we will need to make it available some other way for reference for the inevitable questions. Don't believe anyone when they say, "We won't need that data."

> *Don't believe anyone when they say, "We won't need that data."*

We need to make some data decisions up front. We can defer some data decisions until we get further into the project.

5. Interfaces

In the section on selecting technology, I spoke about how creating interfaces between the new system and other systems is never as easy as the vendors say it will be. Our implementation plan needs to reflect that fact.

One technique is to set up risky interfaces early in the implementation. This is risk mitigation. For example, if we know we will build a web services interface, we should build the prototype early in the implementation to identify potential problems before we are too far along in the project.

By doing it near the beginning of the implementation plan, it gives us time to react to bad news. If we discover some unknown nuance of the interface, we have time to fix it. If we wait until later to build the interface, we won't have that reaction time.

6. Security

Every system we implement has security implications. Modern security needs to assume bad actors are inside our networks. So we need to understand the internal security on any new technology. Modern security best practices require that we set permissions as low as possible to enable each user to do their job.

User authentication needs to integrate with our current authentication process. If we have security down to the data level (e.g., some users can see some data but not others) then that will need to apply to all systems where that data lives. If our reporting system supports row level security, but a new system doesn't, how do we protect the data?

We may need to integrate cloud systems into our security model. For example, if our security model requires tracking of some data changes, will the cloud support that?

For any significant technology, having several security tasks in our implementation plan is important. We need to learn what the built-in security model is, what integration options are viable, and how to verify that we set the security correctly at implementation. Can we regularly audit our security settings to ensure that it is operating as we expect?

7. Test Systems

Any significant system needs to have a test version up and available. We will use this system for training, development, and exploring possibilities.

This step gets tricky when it needs to integrate with other systems. The obvious solution is to integrate it in with other test systems, and this is usually the right move. But license costs and system complexity can make this difficult. For example, external cloud systems don't always include a separate test system.

We also need to learn how to refresh the test system from production to get the most current setup and data. We need to coordinate these updates with the group of users that are using the test system, a group which likely changes over time. We may also need to do the refresh in sync with other test systems if there are interfaces between them.

Some vendors charge extra licenses for test systems. Cloud systems get tricky to integrate with our other test systems. By making sure we understand this as we put our implementation plan together, we can avoid surprises.

8. Support

Most new technology implementations result in questions and problems from the end users. Our training plan discussed above will reduce this a bit, but there is always some ongoing work for the Help Desk.

Make sure the Help Desk gets their hands on the new technology as soon as it is available. Have them involved in some end user training to get a sense for how the new system works.

This is especially true if it is an upgrade from a prior version. As they know the problems the old version has, Help Desk can help identify changes the end users will struggle with.

When we cutover to the new system, the Help Desk should have some expected problems with resolutions, a short FAQ list, and a list of resources for end users.

9. Go Live

Going live with the new system is always an exciting time. Depending on the situation, we have a couple of ways to handle it.

"Big Bang" refers to a hard cutover to the new system at a single point in time. We take an overnight or a weekend and make the cutover. When employees come to work the next day, the new system is in place.

If we choose to run parallel systems, we run the new system and the old system at the same time for a short period. The end users have to do extra work if we expect them to enter data and transactions into both systems. The primary benefit is that we can check for accuracy of the new system while still using the old system. This approach may be used for billing or financial systems.

The last option is the phased implementation. This is a combination of the Big Bang and the parallel-system implementations. Both systems are up and running, but we switch groups of end users over to the new setup at specific times. No specific user has to use both systems at the same time, but the organization is using both systems.

10. Cleanup

During any implementation, we will identify tasks that need to happen after Go Live. If we don't write them down and make time scheduled to take care of them, they won't get done. This is especially true of old servers. Those things seem to stay around like zombies. The temptation to leave the old server up "just in case" will be strong.

Since we likely have virtual servers, shutting down the old system and bringing it back up if needed is straightforward.

Extracting the data from the old system and making it available in spreadsheets, also "just in case", is a way to avoid keeping an old system up and running.

Avoiding this cleanup step will only leave Technical Debt in place (chapter 6) which will cost us money and time down the road.

Get the Implementation Right

From the above list, we can see many places where an implementation can fail. These failures usually have little to do with the product selected. We can try blaming the product instead of the implementation, but that's just not being honest with ourselves.

These failures usually have little to do with the product selected.

Put the time in to select the right product. We also must put the time into the implementation plan or that fine system we selected will end up hated and despised by the organization.

I'll repeat this a third time to drive the point home: A great system, implemented badly, will likely fail. A mediocre system, implemented beautifully, will likely succeed.

CHAPTER 23

TECHNOLOGY WE BUILD

Sometimes we can't buy the technology we need and we need to build it. We need to write custom software that provides unique functionality for our company. Custom software can take a process and make it faster, less error prone, or more efficient.

Custom applications have fallen out of favor in many IT departments. They believe that the costs of custom software do not outweigh the benefits. I think they are correct for most places in an organization. For example, unless we are in an extremely large organization, do we really need anything custom in our accounts payable or receivable department? Probably not. However, the parts of our organization that provide competitive advantage are more likely to benefit from custom applications. Purchased software does not provide lasting competitive advantages.

Another factor driving custom application is the rise of low-code or no-code solutions. These tools provide support for unique workflows in our organizations. They may not create traditional Windows applications, but they still create software functionality that we need to manage.

The last point I will make is that more and more systems are providing robust APIs. Vendors would only do this if they believed there is increasing demand for them. If demand for custom development was dropping, there would be less demand for APIs. I think the vendors are right.

In this chapter, I will discuss the why and how of custom software development. We usually write these applications against a central system, like an ERP or central billing system. While there are many considerations to be aware of when writing custom applications, here are some that have caused my teams the most problems over the years.

When to build our own applications?

Home-grown software has a cost of ownership. The more code we are maintaining, the more staff we need, the longer changes take, and the longer fixes and debugging take. And large bodies of code will always be candidates for rewriting because of changes in business or underlying technology.

Every company I have worked at has had one or two pieces of software written long ago by someone no longer with the company. Everyone pretends it doesn't exist and hopes it doesn't break. But it will need attention someday.

Custom software is not something we want to create casually. It isn't something we want to accidentally start doing. So let's look at the reasons it may make sense for us to head down this path.

ERP and other central systems are large systems developed to work at a variety of companies. They are generic in their approach to support a wide range of situations. The large variety of information and functionality complicates the user interface.

If we have a high transaction area of our company, say, for example, a production floor, the flexibility and extra fields get in the way. Recording time or activity directly into the ERP system can have extra clicks and extra fields that clutter up the view. This can intimidate new employees.

This leads us to our first reason to develop software: Speed. There may be times when we need to minimize the computer interaction to record activity that happens regularly. There may be times when we need to reduce the effort or learning time on a regular task.

It turns out that when we develop for speed, we get the second benefit: Quality. By reducing the effort, the clicks, and the data entry, we can also reduce the possibility of making errors. Sometimes we will develop some software specifically to prevent or to fix errors in our processes. While there is overlap with speed, sometimes we want to create a custom app solely for reducing the errors that are happening.

The last reason we develop custom software is for Differentiation. Something that we do in our organization truly is unique, and an application will allow us to do things that our competitors can't. Think of software that our Customers might use or software that integrates two other systems in a way that allows us to provide products that our competitors can't.

So we have speed, quality, and differentiation. Is that enough to embark on the custom software path? There are some secondary concerns that we need to address:

- Do we have the people to maintain the software? Developers will always need to update the software. If nothing else, the underlying operating systems, databases, or other technologies will change. For every custom piece of software we develop, we are adding to our future work. Custom software lives until we replace it or it is no longer needed. We are making a commitment for future work.

- Can we eliminate or streamline the task instead of writing software for it? We need to review the process being implemented to verify we need it in the future.

- Is there some special knowledge that we are embedding into the custom application that we may end up losing as people change over time? If today's employees have knowledge about the process, but future employees won't need this knowledge because we built it into the application, we must assume this knowledge will disappear. Is that ok?

- Is the technology that is being used going to be around for a while? Development platforms, programming languages, interface techniques, and underlying operating system features are all things that change.

A manufacturer of any decent size must have an ERP system in place. Other industries may have their own central system that serves a similar function. If we decide that we need to write software against the ERP system, there is an important consideration: Extending vs Customizing.

In the simplest terms, *Extending* refers to following the official vendor rules for interfacing with the system. This includes toolsets, languages, APIs, data access mechanisms, and other rules the vendor puts in place. *Customizing* refers to changing the code of the system itself or interfacing in a way that the vendor doesn't officially support.

To put it simply: Extending is good, Customizing is bad. When companies think they are so unique that they should customize the internal workings of the ERP system, there will be future implications, all negative. Upgrades to the ERP system will be more expensive, more complex, and have greater risk. Extending is hard enough as vendors keep updating interfaces, but at least we have a fighting chance of avoiding extra costs and effort for upgrades.

Now that we have decided to build a custom application, let's look a little more at what we need. This won't be a list of technologies, programming techniques, or security techniques. Instead, it is a list of considerations that will make our lives easier.

Leaving Breadcrumbs

The first consideration is to leave ourselves breadcrumbs to follow. Applications get developed and rolled out. If we do a good job of that, we will use the application for a long time — longer than our short-term memory. Ask this question: If we have turnover in the team and user population, and a year from now there is a question or problem with the application, how will we quickly figure out what we need to know to fix the problem?

In the fairy tale Hansel & Gretel, they leave a trail of breadcrumbs on the ground so they can find their way back home. If we can leave digital breadcrumbs, we can find our way back to the original requirements, testing, design, and source code.

I've seen applications that popped up with problems after ten years (!) of quietly being used. They were developed long before we put the current source code system in place. The Help Desk (average turnover of 2-3 years) had no memory or searchable record of the application. They didn't even recognize it as a custom piece of software and spent time on the internet trying to chase down the vendor.

> *If we can leave digital breadcrumbs, we can find our way back to the original requirements, testing, design, and source code.*

While we can't remove all the time bombs that exist in our environments, we can make sure we don't make any new ones. Leaving a trail for the future will do this. Most breadcrumbs are easy and low effort. Here are a few to get us thinking.

- Text on the main UI screen with information about the application. It can be as simple as our company name and some words to make it easier to find the source code. I recommend a version number and release date as this also helps testing and troubleshooting.

- An About page that includes information about the software, such as employees involved in the development, and what problem it was trying to solve. Consider pointing to the location of the error/event log described further in this chapter.

- Keep a list of all applications used and make sure new custom applications get entered. This is also a practice that has uses beyond breadcrumbs. Keeping some information about developers and users also helps.

- If there is a Change Request system or some other method for tracking IT requests, make sure that there is enough information to chase down history when an application raises its head.

- If we have a developer on staff, we will have a new developer someday. Put a bit of documentation in place to help them find their way around things. For example, in the third month of their job, they will need to make an urgent repair on an application they have never seen before. Have mercy on them and leave some breadcrumbs that explain where code is, where the requirements are, who the lead users were, test scenarios, and any design documentation.

- Sometimes, it is our background jobs that throw the error. Rather than just write to the error log (which should still happen), consider emailing the help desk with details about what went wrong and how to fix it. This is very useful for nightly jobs that run successfully most of the time. Put extra information into the email message to reduce the time spent fixing the problem.

Good Source Code Control Practices

Of course, all our source code is in a repository of some sort, right? If not, go do that now and don't come back until it is in place and all custom code is in it. Keeping it in a folder somewhere, or worse, on the developer's computer is like planting land mines in the backyard and not marking them. Something is going to blow up someday.

With our code in a repository, we can move on to some good practices. There are two important ones.

First, we likely have DEV, TEST, and PROD environments for our central system. Don't move executables directly from one environment to the next. Always pull from the repository.

This has several benefits. When we install only from the repository, we know for a fact which code built which executable - there is never any doubt. It cuts down on quick and dirty changes that don't get pushed back into the repository. It also forces all developers to get into good habits regarding installation scripts.

There is sometimes pushback from the developers claiming this is unnecessary work that makes things harder. *"Isn't it more important the application gets put into production quickly? That is too much work."* I would suggest that, once they develop this habit, it adds only minutes to the process and reduces the chances for errors downstream.

Next, put all our database schema changes into scripts. Do not update the schema manually. By putting them into scripts, we reduce the reload effort when we refresh DEV and TEST. If an environment gets refreshed, run the schema scripts and installation scripts and we can get back to our testing.

This one is also straightforward to implement. We need to write code to update the schema, and we will probably need to write an un-update script that removes the changes. We need this because we won't get the script right on the first try, and will need to delete the changes and rerun the script.

Having a schema script as part of our installation helps when we go live, because we know from our testing exactly what needs to change in PROD. This is worth it for any development that changes the database schema.

Testing Testing Testing

Testing custom software is easy because it is custom-built for our specific purpose. It is also hard because we rarely have enough resources to test sufficiently.

Remember our discussion about risk assessment? It applies here as well. If we look at all the things that can go wrong with the application, focusing on how it can affect the business and our Customers, we can put together a test plan that applies our limited resources in the areas most at risk.

There are also a few concepts that we should also consider when putting together our test plan:

- Internal IT testing should focus on the primary function and environmental aspects like permissions, interfaces to other systems, and data integrity. Rarely will IT have the resources to test a new application thoroughly, but all the connections and background setup must be right.

- End user testing should focus on the "happy path" (the primary scenario) and then as many of the exceptions as they can remember. Hopefully, they will have written these down, but in my experience, that is unlikely. The best we can do is continually remind them to update their test plans.

- Chaotic Testing, sometimes called psychotic testing, is a concept that requires a certain personality. Someone needs to sit down with the software and think about how they can break it. They aren't considering normal usage. They are thinking about how to break the assumptions the developers made. They are thinking about how to break the data rules the developers implemented. It takes a special person to think like this, unfortunately; they are hard to find.

- Sanity Tests are a short set of tests that quickly tell us the status of the system. Typically, a sanity test script will only test the "happy path" and the interface connections. They are short and quick to execute. We can use the sanity test scripts for a variety of situations. For example, when a user reports an outage, we can run the sanity test as a quick check to understand if it is just that user or if the outage is more widespread. We can use it to verify the install after an upgrade or each new development build.

The details of our test plans and test results depend on the scale of the change. A large application needs a comprehensive test plan. A small report change won't need as much. Since every delivery of new functionality from IT will need testing, and that testing will be unique to the change, we end up having lots of conversations about test plans.

It is important to keep test plans as simple as possible to make it easier to keep up to date. Very few people like maintaining test plans and our teams will take shortcuts anyway when writing and updating them.

I strongly recommend against a test plan template, as our teams will make all sizes of changes and one template will not fit all. Perhaps, if our organizations do a lot of development, we might think about several test plan templates, but I haven't seen them work, even at the multi-billion dollar companies that did a lot of development.

The templates get rolled out, mandated, and then the exceptions start. After a year or two, the templates get forgotten.

Far better to have continual conversations about test plans with our teams. Point out where we could have caught problems that snuck through into production.

We want to perform all the testing necessary to prevent problems in production, and not a single test more. That is a hard line to figure out, and we won't get it right all the time. Sometimes we will test too much, more often, we won't test enough. There will be some test cases we didn't catch or that the users didn't remember. It is possible to get close to perfect (i.e., no reported bugs ever), but it rarely is worth the extensive testing necessary.

Again, risk assessment (chapter 4) plays a role here. We need to test high-risk scenarios more than low-risk scenarios. I would suggest that the goal of "perfect software" is the wrong goal. The goal should be to balance the testing effort with the expected result. There are certain places where we need to work hard to avoid problems. Some examples would be financial transactions, Customer interactions, and product design automation.

We likely already do this. There is probably not a step in our test plan to go through and verify that there are no typos. There is probably not a step in our test plan to go through and verify that the back button works in all cases. We decide not to document and execute detailed tests on low-risk functionality like fixing a typo on a report we released yesterday.

Here is another scenario. Is it better to spend an extra month testing for perfection or is it better to roll the application out, start getting the benefit for the business, and quickly fix any problems that pop up?

There are costs for the later rollout date. We will incur the opportunity cost of delaying the benefit of the change. We will delay our work on the next project. Delaying for perfection has a cost that we need to be aware of.

Of course, I am not advocating for releasing an application with lots of bugs. I am advocating for a risk-based approach to our test plans and making informed decisions about how deep our testing should go. It isn't easy, but if we learn each time we roll out a new change, we will get better.

Error & Event Logging

Any application of significance will need troubleshooting at some point. During testing, but also once it is in production, there will be times when users report unexpected or problematic behavior. Error and event logging are two techniques to make it easier to figure out what is going on.

I separate event and error logging from each other because they are two distinct functions. The reasons we look in each are different and retention criteria are different. On those rare occasions we simply must have a single list, it is easy to combine them as they both have timestamps.

Error logging captures when a problem occurs. Event logging is used to track when specific activity takes place. While there is some overlap, the different usage scenarios have led me to believe we should implement them as different things.

Once we move out of single developer work and into multi-user testing, keeping track of events becomes useful. We can set the level of event logging to lots of events, only certain events, or just application start. Other events might be screens, transactions, interface information, or data checks.

Error logging captures when a problem occurs. Event logging is used to track when specific activity takes place. While there is some overlap, the different usage scenarios have led me to believe we should implement them as different things.

We can keep the event log in a file or a database, whatever works for our situation. Being able to access it via a spreadsheet gives us the most flexibility when analyzing the entries.

I always start with logging the application startup event. Keep this one when we move the application into production, even if we have turned all other event logging off. By recording when each person starts the application, we know several things:

- We know who is testing or using the application and how frequently.
- We can create a mailing list of people that use the application. This list can be very useful for notifying users of problems, changes, etc. Much better than blasting an email to a larger group because we don't know specifically who is using the application.
- If we are having an intermittent problem (those are the worst), we can turn on logging for particular events to gain a deeper understanding. For example, if the intermittent problem happens when a particular transaction executes, we can turn on logging at that point and dump out lots of variables. The next time it fails, we have more information for troubleshooting.
- If certain permissioned people make changes we need to track for security or audit reasons, we can easily add it to the event log.

Error logs, on the other hand, are for when something goes wrong. Now, we don't want to put something in the error log for when a user enters wrong data, such as text in a number field. The error log is for errors the users can't fix, such as when a system interface throws an error, something triggers a permissions limit, or the database has an internal error.

Such an error will often result in a call to the Help Desk. Having records in the error log will help the troubleshooting process.

Remember the breadcrumbs we talked about earlier? Here is another situation where they can help. If the error is something that needs development help to figure out, putting information into the error log to make it easier to troubleshoot is worth the extra effort.

Here is a list of some information to consider putting into error logs besides the standard date/time, username, and error message displayed to the user:

- Complete sentences explaining what the problem was. There is no excuse for cryptic messages. Have mercy on the person who has to track down the problem.

- The code module that is recording the error.
- The code module that is throwing the error and the parameters in the call to that module.
- Permission sets that may apply.
- The data being worked on. Customer IDs, shop order numbers, part numbers, etc.

The chances of getting a development team to include all of this information for every error are slim. After all, these errors won't happen very often, will they? I look at it as insurance for the inevitable trouble-shooting that will need to take place.

Discover Problems Before Users Do

Speaking of the inevitable troubleshooting, what can we do to prevent the errors from happening? Or discover them before the users do?

Data Integrity

If the system relies on keeping data in sync or on assumptions that data is a certain way, consider having some regular jobs that check and verify our assumptions are true. We can also address this by having some reports that users can run to make sure that the data is as it should be.

Handoffs

When processes move from one department to another, problems can occur at the handoff. Put a check in place, maybe a database trigger or event, that checks to make sure that everything is correct at that point.

This is helpful for catching problems that show up when multiple people are involved. For example, it is straightforward to ensure that data entered on one screen is correct. If fields conflict or options don't match, we can catch it immediately. However, when multiple people are entering information in different areas of the system, we may have a situation where a conflict exists, but the software may not be able to be detect it at data entry.

These may not be a problem in all situations, but bringing potential problems to someone's attention before it becomes an actual problem is often a good idea. Again, reports or event notifications may be the right choice here.

Monitoring

There are several tools on the market, including open source, that watch components of our technology and send alerts when something is amiss. We can use these tools to get alerts when major components go down. Servers, application servers, specific databases, network connections, and storage can be monitored every few seconds.

When something goes wrong, the system notifies the appropriate people immediately via text message and automated phone call. We can also email the Help Desk to give them a heads up.

What this avoids is waiting for our end users to tell us about the problem. When end users report it, there is always the delay to determine if it is just them having the problem or if it is more systemic. Having the monitors in place eliminates that delay.

Point of Need (PON) Help

Help systems and documentation have never gotten the attention they deserve and probably never will. Documentation, if it exists, sits on a shelf or in a folder and doesn't get looked at. If we purchase the software, the help for a field or screen is too generic because the vendor doesn't know the specifics of how our company is using that field or screen. If we wrote the application, it often has no help at all.

The concept of *Point of Need* help is most useful in software we develop. The concept is simple: imagine some point, a single moment in time, when the user is using the software and has a question or doesn't know what to do next. It is at that moment they need to call up help information to figure out what to do next.

The term "contextual help" has been around for a while. However, most implementations have been poor. The help that pops up when entering a field may say something like "Enter the order type" or "Select from the list of order types." No kidding. The user knows how to use a drop-down menu. What they don't know is which order type to choose. PON help would say "[companyname] uses the following order types…" and lists all the types and what we use them for. It would tell the user who to talk to for more information.

PON Help is harder to maintain. Use a simple database call to make it easier to keep updated. Remember, it won't be needed on every field. For example, most people don't need the *Employee* field explained.

PON is also helpful for training new people. If someone new knows that they can just hit a key or click a link whenever it is available and get an explanation, they can self-discover more.

What makes a good PON help screen?

The moment the user tilts their head to the side and goes "Huh?" or "What do I do here?" is where the help needs to be available.

- We write it in business terms for our specific company.
- It provides useful information about how the company does business.
- It can point to a short video that explains things.
- It can point to documentation or people for more information.

A key point in all this is that the moment the user tilts their head to the side and goes "Huh?" or "What do I do here?" is where the help needs to be available.

Other examples of PON help

- A reporting system that has an icon on every report that explains where the data comes from and when the data and the report were last updated, what models and measures where used, and where to go for more information.
- A quick link that brings up the business process and shows where in the process this record is.

Show Your Work (SYW) Screens

By definition, automating a business process means embedding some portion of that process into software. When we embed part of a process into software, we remove that portion from the awareness of the people involved. Users may know the big parts of what the automation does, but there are details about the process that will get lost. There will probably be one or two people from the business that will understand the details of what is going on in the applications, but they will either forget about it over time or will move on to another job.

When we embed part of a process into software, we remove that portion from the awareness of the people involved.

Here is an example. A manufacturing company that relied on their ERP system for look-ahead at production floor loading was not happy with how the ERP system worked. So they changed the code to do deeper analysis of other aspects of the system to determine the best loading. Within three years, the company was again unhappy with it. New leaders and key players had come into the process, and those that designed the original application had left. The organization had forgotten the thinking behind the change.

What had been a fairly well understood glass box system had become a solid box system where people didn't know how the internals worked.

Another example is a food company that had a costing system that was more complex than the ERP could support. They built an application that extracted data from the ERP system and calculated the cost.

After a few years and a few new players, they lost the knowledge about the pricing algorithms. A few people started wondering if it was correct. They would ask, and IT would respond that it was working as designed.

The business user for the initial build of the application was a Spider (chapter 18) so there was a lot of distributed knowledge about the details, especially the edge cases, but no central knowledge of the entire system. When that user moved on to a different company, there was no longer a voice outside IT that could explain how the entire costing application worked and how it generated costs.

Those that distrusted the costing automation started building their own spreadsheets to figure out the costing themselves. They shared the spreadsheet with other people. The spreadsheet handled the normal cases just fine; it even handled one of the edge cases well (the one the spreadsheet creator was knowledgeable about). But it didn't handle everything correctly and sometimes gave wrong information.

However, others didn't know that the spreadsheet had problems and started building pricing off of it. They eventually discovered the errors, and the company had a collective freak-out.

In both the pricing and look-ahead cases, the people that initially specified and validated the application's algorithms were no longer available to explain how the system worked. Since it was an internal application, the documentation put together was not as complete as needed. In one case, the developer still knew how it worked, but no one was asking as they had already bailed on the application and started using spreadsheets.

So what can we do about this problem? How can we embed parts of a process into software, but still keep it visible to the users? To answer that, we will go back to math class. Stay with me here, there is no actual math involved.

Show Your Work is a concept where the automation or calculation steps are visible to the user of the software.

Show Your Work (SYW) is a concept where the automation or calculation steps are visible to the users of the software. Remember math class in school where getting the right answer wasn't good enough? We also had to "show your work" — that is, show the steps we took to get the right answer. It proved to the teacher that we understood the concept. It proved that we knew the process well enough to apply it to a problem.

Show Your Work in an application is the same concept. Consider the costing app I mentioned earlier. Adding a SYW screen allows anyone interested to look and see exactly how the application calculated the cost.

Usually implemented as a separate screen similar to a Help screen, all it needs to do is show the steps that the software took to get to the answer.

A SYW screen should answer the following types of questions. What database query was used to select the record set? What fields were used from those records? What formulas were used to generate new data? What were the variables used in that formula?

In our costing example, the SYW screen might contain:

- Part number in question.
- The entire bill of material for the part, including subassemblies.
- Material and labor costing for each item on the bill of material, showing the labor rates used.
- A list of all cost components with totals.
- A list of the fields used from the ERP system.

One thing that gets tricky about SYW is the additional maintenance task it puts on developers. The developer has to write the code for the algorithm and then document that algorithm again in the SYW section. When updating the algorithm, there are now two places to update.

The benefit of SYW is that there is now a data or process debugging tool built right in the application for everyone to see. The developer and the business can use this to verify that the application is performing correctly. This is handy during the initial release, but also several years down the road when people forget how the system works. Or when new people join the company and question if the software is doing things right.

> *The benefit of SYW is that there is now a data or process debugging tool built right in the application for everyone to see.*

Putting a SYW screen into an application helps the business understand how the application works. It can be part of training to show a new employee the details of a process. Maybe it also shows them what the underlying data is and how it all ties together.

Let's look at the production floor look-ahead example with a SYW screen. It would show the following items:

- The part being ordered and the quantity.
- All the operation steps involved.
- Any subassemblies involved.
- The production centers involved with machine and labor requirements of the part and the availability of those resources.
- The production floor loading on the various dates checked.
- Calculations and results for the final date and loadings.

Here is another example where we implemented SYW.

In the packaging department, there was frequent design work that required a lot of small, very detailed work. The work was tedious and time-consuming. An old application existed to help, but they built it on design software that was past the date of last support and the vendor wouldn't help at all. The people that built the application had scattered to the winds. And this was years ago, so their memory wouldn't be helpful even if we could find them.

So we needed to build a new application.

There was concern from the package designers that this was all very complicated and IT people, much less an outside contractor, could never understand the complexities enough to write the new application. To make matters worse, the new application needed to interface with brand-new design software that the packaging department was implementing at the same time.

This application would have a lot of math in it. It would have calculations for many sizes and shapes. There were lots of calculations for positioning that depended on the shape of other components in the design.

The SYW page for this tool became a critical part of proving that the software was working correctly. The developer and package designer used it as a common communication language as they worked through the development. It supported iterative development better because the user could see the algorithm steps on the SYW screen.

With that tool in place for a while now, the current user base still understands how the system works and has somewhere to go check when they wonder if something is correct. The SYW page has saved countless hours of user and developer time by exposing the algorithm and the data behind it. It also forced the developer to show their work and not take shortcuts in the algorithm.

There is one further extension of the SYW concept that I haven't had the chance to implement yet. I call it *Show Your Reasoning*.

The idea is to, like SYW, have a place where the user can go to see the reasoning, the thinking behind the automation. See the design goals and business motivations for the software tool's creation. *Show Your Reasoning* would include what assumptions the developer made and maybe some information about the business goal for automation.

At first glance, this looks like embedding the entire requirements document into the application. And the slide show that explained the rationale for building the application. While that would be ideal, it isn't workable. But there are probably a few key points from those documents that are worth putting in.

Think of a *Show Your Reasoning* screen as answering this question: Why does this application exist?

This would help document the reasons for the application's existence. If those assumptions or goals change, the people working the process today — remember that they are rarely the ones that built the software in the first place — can see and verify if all of it is still true.

This idea comes out of my experience that, because of employees leaving or changing jobs, organizations forget those initial goals, assumptions, and requirements. Once they forget it, the application no longer is useful. People don't trust what they don't understand, and the application may do more harm than good.

While I believe that the need for organizations to build custom applications to stay competitive is increasing, it is not without risk. In many cases, it is better to change our processes to match our central system. However, in situations where it provides a competitive advantage, we should give it serious thought.

CHAPTER 24

SHADOW IT

Shadow IT is a hot topic in many organizations. Or at least IT thinks it is a hot topic. To be more specific, many in IT think that Shadow IT is evil and is a problem we need to prevent. There may have been one or two of you that, seeing this chapter in the table of contents, flipped to it first thing.

I agree it is a problem, a big one in some organizations. But it is not a problem we need to stamp out completely, like a disease. Rather, it is a symptom we need to understand. And it is an activity that we need to manage, not eradicate.

In fact, it isn't hard to turn it into a force for good in our organization. In this chapter, I will present some ideas for how to do this.

According to Wikipedia, at the time of writing, Shadow IT refers to information systems that are built and deployed by departments other than the IT department because of shortcomings of the central information systems.

I would add a couple of things to this definition before we discuss whether Shadow IT is the source of all good or evil in IT today (spoiler: it is neither).

There is always a gap between how good of a job we think we are doing and what the organization perceives. The speed of IT will frustrate those that don't have the top priority projects. This gap has been at every company I have worked for and heard about. The gap may be big or small, it may grow or shrink. Upper management may be concerned or not. But the gap is real and we will never eliminate it.

This gap provides a motive for Shadow IT.

The ever-changing technology world provides the means.

Many products on the market make it easier for people to develop applications, reports, and other integrated systems. The line between consumer and IT technology is blurring.

And the vendors aren't necessarily friends of IT. Look at how many of them promote the fact that "no IT help is needed." Look at the vendors that take credit cards to get started "quickly and easily." Why are the vendors doing this? Because their job is to design and sell product, not to make the IT department look good. That doesn't make them evil or the enemy.

Let's look at the kinds of things happening with Shadow IT. We won't see all of these in our companies, but we likely will see a few of them.

Getting data out of our systems and into reports or analytic tools is rapidly changing. Spreadsheets used to be the only thing to worry about, but now there are all kinds of tools from small and large vendors to make data analyzing much easier to set up and use. Many "no code" tools are on the market that allow for interactive reporting. Spreadsheets have only gotten worse as a new generation of employees have grown up with them, and they see them as a fundamental tool to use.

Application development is becoming easier. Tools that allow for building sequences of tasks with data access can mimic full applications. Web development is becoming much simpler. The ability for an employee to create a small application with no programming knowledge is increasing and will continue to do so.

In some larger companies, departments are going around IT and directly bringing in products and developers to build systems they can't get in a timely fashion from the IT department.

Shadow IT is real. And we can't stop it.

Ok, back to your objections. You have already started the list of problems with Shadow IT in your head. But let's look at a few more points. There are more positives than we might think;

- Is this really where we want our non-IT people to be spending their time? At first glance, we answer no, as they have their normal job to do. But if they can spend a week creating something that saves a hundred weeks in their department, is that such a bad thing?

- IT works on the top priority tasks for the company, and the department only built this little application because it wasn't a top priority item and would never get done. Well, IT is doing the top priority work, that's good, right? Yes, but. Be careful here. If change requests stop coming in because "IT is too slow" or "Nothing gets done through IT," then IT becomes completely out of the loop. Going around IT becomes the norm, regardless of any management mandate.

- Departments will do product research, including contacting vendors without IT involvement. Do we know why? Possibly, it is a new employee with their own ideas. Or perhaps the current solution is missing something significant and the relationship between that department and IT is not strong enough to support a frank conversation. Are we really hearing the complaints from the rest of the organization? Can we state their issues clearly enough so they know we understand them?

- IT creates an architecture for delivering functionality, and Shadow IT doesn't follow that. This one is true, and there isn't much good about it. It can cause security or data integrity problems.

- It is usually one person who creates a Shadow IT application. While that person is around, they provide support. They answer questions and make tweaks as needed. When they leave, however, support disappears entirely. There have been several times in my career when orphaned Shadow IT applications have shown up on IT's doorway, needing care and feeding. No documentation.

No understanding of how it was built. And in a couple of cases, no source code.

- Shadow IT doesn't get updated for operating system or infrastructure changes. Most organizations have at least one application they haven't updated to support newer operating systems or hardware. This can hold up operating system upgrades or result in another orphan at IT's door.

- Security is often a secondary concern of Shadow IT. It doesn't integrate into the access control and identity management systems that exist. Cloud systems are completely standalone from the rest of IT's architecture and often have their own security. This results in double work to control access.

- The Shadow IT application and its data may not be backed up anywhere. This, of course, becomes an IT problem when something goes wrong.

- If there is source code, it isn't in the repository. It likely lives in a folder on the employee's computer. Hopefully backed up. If the employee changes jobs or leaves the company, the source code is at risk.

- The department gets functionality they need quickly and designed just for them. And they get it faster than if they waited for us in IT. In the end, this is the primary benefit and the principal reason that Shadow IT exists. And it is hard to argue with. The department used technology to improve a business process. They just didn't use our team to get it done.

I believe that there can be a more constructive approach to Shadow IT. One that understands and accepts its existence and works with everyone to make it into a force for good in the company. Let's look at a couple of scenarios that move us in this better direction.

Sometimes, it makes sense for a prototype to verify that a process improvement is going to do what we need. If a department can mock up an application and try it out, they can get a better sense of what the requirements should be. In the best case, the conversation goes something like this: *"Hey, IT, we wrote an application that makes our process faster. We want you to build a real version of it."*

When this happens, the requirements and workflow improvements are better understood by the business. This can help reduce scope creep and missing requirements. The users may have a specific solution in mind that is not the best, but at least the conversation can start with a good set of requirements.

Another benefit, especially in data reporting and analysis products, is letting new ideas pop up and take hold. IT never has time to learn all the tools that come out. But if an employee is especially driven to experiment with something that can help their job, the organization can still gain this knowledge and move forward as appropriate.

When PowerBI first came out, non-IT employees were the first ones to play with it. They came up with some interesting ideas that IT then built into the common systems.

So what can we do to leverage Shadow IT instead of fighting it? Shadow IT is going to happen. If we view it as only a problem and something we need to eradicate, we will hurt our companies.

There are a few key things we can do to turn Shadow IT into a positive:

- Create a data repository focused on reporting and analysis that enables self-service for spreadsheets and other popular tools. Having a central set of validated data models will ensure that everyone is looking at the same data and measures. This makes sure that everyone is using the same definition for scrap, revenue, or other terms. When new reporting tools sneak in, at least they will go against common data models.

- Document the architecture and make it available to anyone that asks. This should not be a document that is just tossed at the requester through email and forgotten about. We know the areas that are likely to have Shadow IT. Be proactive about getting the architecture information into their heads with conversations, presentations, and other communications. This becomes the roadmap for doing Shadow IT the right way.

- Ensure the basic security model is available to anyone. Instructions on how to hook into Active Directory (or whatever) properly can go a long way to making sure that fewer security risks get added to the environment. If we can design it so they need a simple token or key to connect, and IT hands those tokens out without a lot of red tape and approvals, we enable basic security and we know who is developing these applications.

- Have discussions with upper management to ensure that they understand our approach. Presenting a good understanding of the pros and cons of Shadow IT shows that IT wants to make sure we do it correctly. If IT does not frame the Shadow IT discussion in a balanced way, we come across as just protecting our turf and not part of the solution. The best message to convey is IT understands and supports Shadow IT when individuals do it the right way.

> *The best message to convey is IT understands and supports Shadow IT when individuals do it the right way.*

Chapter 25

WHEN WE DON'T NEED TECHNOLOGY

It may seem strange to end an IT book with a chapter on when we don't need technology. But looking back on the Business and People parts of the book, it shouldn't be a surprise that we can't improve everything with technology. It is just as important to know when technology is not the answer.

So keep an eye out for those places where technology shouldn't be part of the solution. As the leader of the IT department, we risk the old adage: "When we have a hammer, everything looks like a nail."

The human brain is a funny thing, and sometimes manually doing some tasks produce different human responses than clicking on the computer and getting the results.

Here are some examples I have come across where collecting and analyzing data manually works better than automation.

Front line Production Floor Metrics.

Let's look at two methods. One method is printing out results from yesterday and posting them on the board. Another is hand writing results during the day. Which will be better to drive action? In most cases, the goals (less scrap, more throughput) translate to action better when we write the results as we go through the day than if we merely printed out as a report and posted it.

The pride and the urge to get better comes from writing our results in front of our peers. If it comes from a printout, it is more anonymous, and we can dispute the numbers easier than we can our own handwriting.

Yes, it may be less efficient than printing out a report. However, it is easy to keep the manual recording to a minimum while still getting the benefits. And the benefits of greater ownership of the results can offset the lower efficiency.

We can dispute printed numbers easier than we can our own handwriting.

Production Assignments.

On manufacturing production floors, we may move people between different areas. Product demand shifts, requiring more people in a certain area than last week. People take vacations and get sick, and supervisors need to find others to cover their jobs.

We base the decisions of where to move people on training, experience, aptitude, speed of learning, and other factors. These are hard to quantify into a computer system.

Handwritten whiteboards are common on many production floors. Names and assignments are written down and updated as needed.

These whiteboards provide a larger area for viewing than any printout. Erasing and writing names is almost always easier than updating a computer system. Supervisors and employees can see at a glance where everyone should be.

If people's names are on a magnetic strip, it is even easier to move them around. If someone is sick, they get moved to the edge of the board and the hole is obvious.

This kind of physical manipulation (writing or moving) helps the supervisors keep a comprehensive understanding of what is happening with their people.

It would be very difficult to build a computer application that would take into account all the factors that go into decisions to move people. The best we can do is to provide additional information that may not be on the boards.

For example, if we track time, we know what areas people have worked in and can provide a glimpse into the experience people have. This can help supervisors identify candidates when they need to fill in a hole. But this is a long way from automating the entire process.

Initial Thinking around Metrics

The last example I want to cover is doing the initial work when creating a new metric. Starting with a spreadsheet helps us understand the data behind the metric better. We can play with various formulas and visualizations to determine which ones will work best. Once we see the metric over time, we can easily make changes without getting a developer or report writer involved. Bring the technology in after we have worked out the metric manually.

The trend is towards more technology in the organization. However, not everything needs technology and we need to take care to not assume otherwise.

Part 5

Final Thoughts

Leading the IT department is a tough but rewarding, job. It is a challenge to stay on top of the complexities of Business, People, and Technology. I've covered a lot of topics in this book. Not all of them will resonate with you, but some of them will.

If you are an existing IT Leader, perhaps you have learned a fresh way of thinking about some old problems. If you are hoping to be an IT leader, you may return to this book over your career to revisit topics as your experience grows.

Nothing is ever static in an organization. Scan back over the table of contents and notice how many of the chapters discuss the journey, not the end.

The job of leading the IT department is one of leading an expedition on a journey through a badly mapped out world. I hope that I have given you some tools to better navigate.

Best of luck on your journey!

Acknowledgments

First, I would like to thank Joyce, my amazing wife. She encouraged and supported me throughout all of this, listening as I went on and on...and on and on...about this or that arcane point or how I should organize a particular section. She is my anchor and my springboard.

The *Ex-Libres II* Writers Group was a great place to introduce several of these chapters and help me find my voice.

I especially want to thank my Alpha Reader Team: Mike Wasik, Renee Heinbuch, Jeff Strang, Cynthia Daigle, and Mark Mullozzi. These are leaders in the IT field that were gracious enough to help. Their insight and feedback was invaluable in finalizing the organization and tone of the book.

K.M. Herkes (dawnrigger.com) provided timely helpful tips that helped my understanding of the byzantine publishing world.

QUOTES

2: If I had this book at the beginning of my IT career, I would have made far fewer mistakes.

4: Let's get started.

12: I think it helps us approach change in any project by understanding what we can control, what we can't control, and how people consider change.

20: Focus on the most important tasks. Completely finish the project before moving on to the next one.

22: There will always be a bottleneck somewhere in our department. If not, we are over-staffed.

32: Make the risk less likely to happen. Make the risk less severe if it happens. And make it easier to detect when the risk happens.

33: We don't need to become an expert on risk assessment, we just need to know enough to apply the principles to our job.

36: Proactivity is important, and we should strive to do more of it. However, I believe that proactivity is overrated and insufficient.

37: How many times have we criticized past decisions of ourselves or someone else?

41: The ability of our company to respond quickly to changes and opportunities will determine its success.

44: The fastest ticket to solve is the one that doesn't happen.

52: Technical Debt is a reality for us. We can't prevent it. All we can do is to be aware of it and the future costs from it, and do our best to minimize it.

57: If you have a weak understanding of the business, you will fail as an IT leader.

64: Given the choice of having IT staff learn the business or learning technology, I prefer they learn the business. This is especially true in the applications group.

65: I believe an excellent team of Business Analysts will know the business processes better than any other department in the organization.

67: The responsibility is not with the rest of the company to believe IT understands the business. The responsibility is on us to show that we understand it.

69: For each department, we should know what is important to them and what they are trying to change or improve.

70: Our most important job is to look outside our department at the larger organization.

74: The word "customer" should never denote internal business partners or departments.

85: The only reason to categorize the exceptions is to reduce them.

92: The reboot doesn't fix the problem, it only masks it. But sometimes, rebooting and calling it good is the right thing. Just not too often, ok?

96: Think of Change Requests as all the changes the business needs IT to implement to improve a business process.

101: Having a long list of things to do and no sense of prioritization is a recipe for wasted time.

108: Opportunity cost is understanding the cost of what they are not working on.

113: It would be ideal if there was no IT prioritization list, if the IT prioritization was simply the organization's priority list.

114: IT is so busy making everyone else's processes better that we don't take time to improve our own processes.

119: With talented people and mediocre technology, we can still make a big impact on the company's success.

122: We control our devices, don't let it be the other way around.

124: We don't have to do everything that the organization asks of us. We need to do the things the organization needs of us.

125: We often encourage monkeys to jump from the employee's shoulder to our shoulder.

129: Some decisions are the dog, and some decisions are the tail. The dog always wags the tail, the tail never wags the dog.

130: Asking questions from a place of genuine curiosity usually results in people sharing about their job, what's going well and not so well, and their ideas and opinions.

133: I believe that a core component of leading people is to understand and leverage their strengths.

136: The first time we swallow our words and accept something different from what we would have done is the first time we trust our team.

140: Positive feedback is critical for driving any change.

149: Like plywood made of thin sheets of wood with different orientations, a team is stronger when the parts are not all the same.

156: Each person who submits a resume is a real live person with hopes and dreams.

157: I believe that both leadership styles are necessary in a company.

158: Spiders know an immense amount about their area of the organization. They know the people, processes, and data in great detail.

159: A Conductor in an organization understands how the overall business runs, how processes move between departments, and what affects the pacing and speed of the company.

160: Spiders connect with individuals. Conductors connect with groups. Spiders know how individuals should work together. Conductors know how groups should work together.

161: Outstanding leaders are always looking for other leaders.

165: Time & Materials projects are much better than fixed bid.

175: The key is knowing how to select and integrate technologies into the company so that the organization, and the people in it, can succeed.

177: It comes down to understanding the outline of technology, the impact of technology on the organization, and the ability to learn quickly.

182: We have a responsibility to leave the organization in better shape than we found it, regardless of whether the technology portfolio is shiny and fresh or a haphazard mix of old and new.

184: I am strongly in the IT-only camp for bringing in new technology. The resulting consistency of the portfolio is the clearest benefit.

189: If leadership understands the journey, and the reasoning behind it, they won't stop believing in it.

191: A great system, implemented badly, will likely fail. A mediocre system, implemented beautifully, will likely succeed.

193: The vendor will claim the interface can do anything we want. But until we write some prototype code that proves otherwise, we must assume it will not match what we need.

195: Products and technologies have a current state, but are never static.

202: Every piece of technology we bring into our company has intangible costs of people's time and impact on other technologies. It is the intangible costs that can cause the most problems for us.

210: Don't believe anyone when they say, "We won't need that data."

213: These failures usually have little to do with the product selected.

218: If we can leave digital breadcrumbs, we can find our way back to the original requirements, testing, design, and source code.

223: Error logging captures when a problem occurs. Event logging is used to track when specific activity takes place. While there is some overlap, the different usage scenarios have led me to believe we should implement them as different things.

227: The moment the user tilts their head to the side and goes "Huh?" or "What do I do here?" is where the help needs to be available.

228: When we embed part of a process into software, we remove that portion from the awareness of the people involved.

229: Show Your Work is a concept where the automation or calculation steps are visible to the user of the software.

230: The benefit of SYW is that there is now a data or process debugging tool built right in the application for everyone to see.

238: The best message to convey is IT understands and supports Shadow IT when individuals do it the right way.

240: We can dispute printed numbers easier than we can our own hand-writing.

243: Best of luck on your journey!

Names from the Examples

As you might expect, I have changed the names of the people in the examples. Since I had no intention of using last names, I focused on first names.

Rather than pick them randomly, I picked interesting people from history. There is no connection between the particular story and the individuals listed below.

- **Marie**: Marie Van Brittan Brown patented the closed-circuit security system.
- **Elijah**: Elijah McCoy had 57 patents, many around locomotive lubrication, including a folding ironing board and a lawn sprinkler.
- **Alice**: Alice H. Parker patented the natural gas central heating furnace.
- **Alex**: Alexander Miles patented the safety auto-close elevator doors.
- **Lonnie:** Lonnie Johnson held over 70 patents, including the Super Soaker toys.

About the Author

John Bredesen has worked in IT since the 1980s at large and small companies with vastly different budget priorities. Within IT, John has been a system administrator, a developer, a business analyst, a manager, and a director. There is little he hasn't experienced.

John also worked outside of IT for eight years in project and product management. In this role, he was a consumer of IT services, which gives him a unique perspective on the role of IT in an organization.

When not at work or writing, John lives in St. Paul, MN with his wife, enjoying grandkid visits and the wildlife wandering through the backyard. He also has an intense love of music. While he rebelled against piano lessons as a kid and never had the discipline to practice as an adult, he has a stupidly extensive music collection.

If you like this book, head on over to his website and join the mailing list to stay up to date. John promises to keep the signal-to-noise ratio high and the Rush references low.

https://johnbredesen.com/
https://the-it-director.com/

www.ingramcontent.com/pod-product-compliance
Lightning Source LLC
Chambersburg PA
CBHW071551210326
41597CB00019B/3201